EPIC AIR FRYER HEALTHY COOKBOOK

100 INCREDIBLY GOOD VEGETARIAN RECIPES THAT TAKE PLANT-BASED AIR FRYING IN AMAZING NEW DIRECTIONS

Michelle Anderson

HARVARD COMMON PRESS

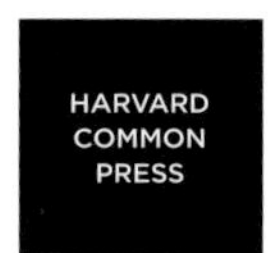

Brimming with creative inspiration, how-to projects, and useful information to enrich your everyday life, Quarto Knows is a favorite destination for those pursuing their interests and passions. Visit our site and dig deeper with our books into your area of interest: Quarto Creates, Quarto Cooks, Quarto Homes, Quarto Lives, Quarto Drives, Quarto Explores, Quarto Gifts, or Quarto Kids.

First Published in 2021 by The Harvard Common Press, an imprint of The Quarto Group,
100 Cummings Center, Suite 265-D, Beverly, MA 01915, USA.
T (978) 282-9590 F (978) 283-2742 QuartoKnows.com

25 24 23 22 21 1 2 3 4 5

ISBN: 978-0-7603-7119-0

Design and Layout: Cindy Samargia Laun
Photography: Glenn Scott
Photography Styling: Natasha Taylor

About the Author
Michelle Anderson was a chef for twenty years before devoting herself to food writing and becoming a widely admired cookbook author. She uses natural and healthy—yet easy-to-find—ingredients in her recipes. She has also written *Making Artisan Breads for the Bread Machine*, *Clean Eating Weeknight Dinner Plan*, and *Healthy Cookbook for Two*. She lives in Ontario, Canada.

Printed in China

To my husband, Scott,
and my sons, Mac and Cooper

Sides ▪ 96

Main Courses ▪ 112

Desserts and Baked Things ▪ 154

INTRODUCTION

Healthy Air Frying

Doesn't it seem like there is a new "must-have" kitchen device available every time you turn around? Advertisements, blog posts, and celebrity endorsements pile up, creating a frenzy to own said appliance because it will change your life, save you time, or create food that is otherwise out of reach. So, you cave in and buy one, and unless the device is exceptional and lives up to the marketing, it is soon relegated to a dark kitchen cupboard or dusty corner of the basement in a sad appliance graveyard. Some appliances are shining exceptions that become valuable additions to your daily routine and carve out a coveted space on your kitchen counter. The air fryer is one of these exceptions; it is efficient, easy to master, and does everything promised and more.

I am a relative latecomer to the air fryer brigade. I had too many other appliances that did not make the cut, and, as a chef, I was admittedly a wee bit snobby and skeptical of the hype. Plus, fried foods weren't standard fare in my daily kitchen routine, so why would I need something to make french fries and mozzarella sticks? In hindsight, my rationalizations for avoiding air fryers were flawed, and after creating many different types of cuisine in the device, I will admit I was wrong. I do need an air fryer, especially for the delicious, plant-based meals my family prefers.

I am a recent empty nester whose strapping, apparently bottomless sons moved out, leaving me still preparing heaps of food for my husband and myself. It is challenging to switch culinary gears to smaller meals, especially in the pursuit of healthy options rather than convenience. Reducing recipe size does not equal less time or effort, so I needed a cooking method that produced high-quality, tasty food with little supervision and in less time. Enter the air fryer. The small size is ideal for two people, and my kitchen remained cool and comfortable even after almost constant use, testing, and tweaking of the fabulous recipes for this book. I can tell you: air fryers are not just for convenience foods or fried foods; you can make full meals—Goat Cheese Breakfast Pizzas (page 25), Barbecue Tofu and Mango Sandwiches (page 48), North African Tagine (page 123), and Pumpkin Lentil Curry (page 121). You can even bake a Chocolate Chili Cake (page 159) or Southern Peach Mini Pies (page 156) for a special occasion (or to eat the cake directly out of the baking dish with your fingers while it is too hot, like my husband).

Many recipe resources for air fryers focus on foods such as fried chicken and breaded shrimp, but this appliance can create incredible plant-based foods as well. The recipes in this book are not all standard fried foods. I tried to include cuisine from all over the world, so your experience is well-rounded and you get an idea of the possibilities of the air fryer. You will find casseroles, soups that use air-fried components, pasta, "meatballs," and sandwiches among the expected wontons, tostadas, and fries. Some of these dishes are vegan or can be converted to vegan with a couple substitutions. Plant-based foods turn out spectacular in an air fryer, but some vegan cheeses and other products do not react the same way as "regular" ingredients. You probably already know the best choices for melting and for sauces, so use your judgment. The times and temperatures are calculated for the air fryer sitting in my kitchen, a Ninja model with 4-quart capacity. Your air fryer might take longer or shorter to cook the recipes, and temperature might vary a few degrees in either direction. Experiment to get the ideal results for your model, and have some fun!

Tuscan Eggs with Sundried Tomato page 34

Getting Acquainted

You might already have an air fryer or perhaps have picked up this book in preparation for purchasing one of these handy devices; whatever the reason, getting familiar with all aspects will only improve your recipe results.

What Is an Air Fryer?

Just to be clear, there is no frying going on in the chamber of an air fryer; the circulating hot air just mimics the oil-based cooking method. Air fryers will give you a similar crunchy "fried" finish without dunking the food in hot, smelly oil. You will need to add very little oil for stellar results. So, if this device is not frying, what on earth does it do? What you see sitting on your counter is basically a mini convection oven, and a powerful one for its size. If you are familiar with cooking in a standard convection oven, you know food cooks faster and browns up beautifully. Air fryers use similar technology in a smaller space using a fan, heating element, and perforated basket to swirl hot air rapidly all around the food—from top to bottom—browning and crisping every side efficiently. Like a convection oven, the fan and exhaust combination in the small air fryer sucks moisture away from the surface of food, so reheated products such as pizza are never soggy, and moist vegetables such as zucchini and eggplant caramelize beautifully. The powerful fan also whips the oil droplets brushed or sprayed on food around the chamber to create that signature fried-food texture and look, while the interior remains juicy and moist. Depending on the model, air fryers can also roast, bake, and reheat foods, along with other functions such as dehydrating. All this without heating up your kitchen, not bad for a small countertop appliance.

Benefits Associated with Air Frying

So, you probably did a little research on this device before purchasing it (or you may be an experienced user already), but it is never a bad thing to look at the benefits of air frying. Most people pick up an air fryer because cooking with less oil is healthier, or because fried foods are a favorite choice but dealing with gallons of oil is not ideal, especially old smelly oil; no one knows how to get rid of that conveniently. Obviously, health and convenience are a win-win, but there are more benefits you might not have considered.

Convenient and Compact

I do not have a large kitchen, and my counter space is premium real estate. When not in use, my air fryer tucks away in an area too small to put anything else except maybe the coffeemaker. I just move it next to my stovetop when I need it, preheat the device in minutes, and usually have dinner on the table in less than twenty minutes. This expends less energy—so saves me money—and I do not have to bend over to take anything out of the regular oven. Plus, clean-up is a snap! (See page 14.)

Healthier than Deep-Frying

It should not come as a shock that immersing food in hot oil to cook it is not healthy. Unfortunately, fried food is also crispy, golden, and has an incredible yummy taste, as my mother would have said, so people overlook the added calories and fat. Deep-frying is also linked to cancer because it can produce carcinogens such as acrylamide. You can cook traditionally deep-fried foods in your air fryer with little or no oil, get almost identical results, and reduce your exposure to acrylamide.

Less Supervision

I am a chef, so multitasking is second nature, but I don't want to be tied to a stove when other tasks need to be done. Deep-frying in particular needs to be supervised and is messy. I love putting food into the air fryer and walking away. Some foods do need turning or shaking, but the hands-on time is limited. The appliance has a built-in timer, and the unit turns off when the time is complete, so the chances of overdone food are slim. I also use a manual timer for extra control (page 13).

Odorless

When I worked in commercial kitchens that contained a deep fryer, my husband requested I sleep on the couch on days we blanched the battered fish or chicken wings because the smell of the oil clung to me, even after long showers. So, the built-in filter in the air fryer is much appreciated—no oil smells wafting through the house or settling in my hair or clothes.

Reduced Cooking Times

Air fryers are speedy; cooking times are reduced by about 30 percent. This is particularly important to know if you convert your own recipes. The small cabinet and the swirling hot air mean it heats up quickly and food is ready faster, even frozen food.

Versatile

Air frying does not just mean fried foods. My basic model has other settings, and I make recipes traditionally pan-fried, baked, roasted, sautéed, and braised. This book deliberately presents recipes that are not fried foods to show the versatility of this kitchen appliance. Breaded items turn out beautifully, grilled cheese sandwiches are a dream, and when I tested the Chocolate Chili Cake (page 159), the texture was so velvety, we ate the whole thing right out of the cake pan. The best way to gauge your air fryer's performance is to experiment, so jump in and enjoy!

Your Kitchen Stays Cool

I live in northern Canada, where the seasons are distinct, so summer can be scorching. We live on salads and sandwiches or barbecue, because turning on the oven or stovetop creates sauna-like conditions in the kitchen. And my husband complains about the extra cost of air conditioning. The air fryer was the perfect solution to expand our diet in hot weather. The unit's sides can get hot, and it does vent through the top, but the heat does not spread beyond a few inches.

So, are there drawbacks to this fabulous cooking device, or is it all moonlight and roses? If you are feeding a large family, an air fryer will most likely not produce enough food. It is a small appliance, perfect for singles and couples. You can make the side dish, appetizer, or even the entrée (depending on the model) and save oven or stovetop space. Also, making some foods in the air fryer can take more time than a deep fryer, such as fries, but the convenience, lack of mess, and healthier finished product are worth the extra minutes.

Choosing Your Air Fryer

If you have not yet purchased an air fryer, there are many factors to consider before making your choice. Think about exactly what you would like the air fryer to do for you. What is your budget? How much space is available in your kitchen? Will you be moving the air fryer around, or will it stay in one place? How many people will you be feeding? What cooking functions do you need?

Let's talk about the budget. This is probably the defining factor when considering an air fryer, because if you can only afford a smaller basic unit—which will work perfectly fine for every recipe in this book—then looking at the larger ones is a waste of your time. Air fryers cost between $70 and $500, with the average unit costing about $100, so there is a model for most people. Basic units are often smaller, with manual dials, and the exhaust fan can be quite loud, but they will produce the same quality food (or close enough that it is not noticeable). So, decide your budget and research affordable air fryers.

If you plan on keeping the unit on the counter, measure the space the air fryer will live in and subtract 5 inches (13 cm) on all sides. That final number will be the maximum size possible for the unit. If you plan to store the air fryer when not in use, consider the weight you will be toting around and what space you have for storage. Most air fryers are ideal for preparing food for two to four people, and even then, you might have to cook in batches depending on the recipe and size of the unit. If your family is large, air fryers are not the best choice for creating full meals.

Now, what are the differences between the various models? The original air fryer design looks like an egg and has a detachable basket/bucket on the bottom. This style can range in size from 2-quart baskets to almost 10 quarts, marketed as a "family-size" appliance. I have a smaller egg-shaped unit, which I used for creating the recipes in this book. The basket contains a removable perforated insert that elevates the food; this piece is used in every recipe in this book.

There are also toaster oven–style air fryers—I have one of these too—that are bigger and usually have several other settings beyond air frying. These appliances are typically more expensive and utilize a tray and mesh basket combination to allow for airflow during the air-fry program. The mesh basket is hard to clean; you will need to soak it and use a brush to remove the food bits.

The price of either style is influenced by its different bells and whistles, such as controls, pre-sets, or programs. Dial controls work well, but you might want to manually time the cooking with your watch or phone to be more precise. More expensive units often have digital time and temperature controls. Pre-set programs for fries, roasted vegetables, and eggs can be handy if you know these foods are regular additions to your meals; otherwise, it is just as easy to put in the time and temperature you need manually. Programs are where you will see the most significant differences between air fryers as well as between egg-shaped and toaster-oven types. The basic model I use most has Air Fry, Roast, Dehydrate, and Reheat on the control panel. More expensive units can also have Convection Bake, Convection Broil, Broil, Bake, Rotisserie, Pizza, Grill, and Toast on the panel.

What else will affect the price when buying your air fryer? Some of the little extras you can consider are these:

- Paddles that stir the food
- A viewing window to check the food without opening the unit
- Controls that shut off the unit when you open it and restart when you close it; or button controls to stop the cooking process
- The ability to connect to apps, so you can control the appliance from your phone or tablet
- Multiple compartments or extra cooking racks that cook different foods at the same time
- Rotating baskets on a tilted angle with a rotating bowl that tumble the food for even cooking
- Dishwasher-safe parts for easy clean-up
- Top- or front-opening units (if the area where you want to run the appliance has limited space above the unit, a top opening lid is not convenient)
- Accessories you will need to make the foods you want, and whether these fit in the unit

AIR FRYER ACCESSORIES

Cool accessories for your air fryer can be found online and in most kitchen stores, some designed specifically for this device and others that can be used effectively for your recipes.

- **Accessory kit:** These packages include many of the most popular tools and pans for an attractive price. You can choose which kit suits your needs best.
- **Bundt pan:** These don't always fit in every air fryer, but you can find 8½-inch (21.5 cm) pans that will be fine for larger air fryers.
- **Grill pan:** This is a round, nonstick pan, with a raised grid and holes to let any fat drip down. It is lovely for vegetables, veggie burgers, and sandwiches.
- **Mandoline:** This device slices, dices, and creates pretty waffle-patterned vegetables for all your recipe needs.
- **Muffin pan:** These can be either silicone or metal and usually have six cups in the tray. This accessory fits most air fryers.
- **Oil sprayer:** To avoid using aerosol cooking oil spray, invest in a hand pump sprayer filled with olive oil or vegetable oil.
- **Parchment paper liners:** These are conveniently the right size and have small holes to facilitate airflow. Perfect for preventing your food from sticking. Make sure your food items hold the paper down, or it can blow around.

Air Fryer Tips and Hacks

My little air fryer experienced extensive use while I was testing the recipes for this book, and I have gained a real respect for its capabilities. Does everything turn out perfect? No, the finished product was dependent on the baking dish's size, the type of ingredient, seasoning, timing, and oil. You will also have to consider the model of air fryer, because they all produce different results. Start with the timing and temperature used in this book and tweak it for your own unit. When possible, cook one item first, such as one egg, one wonton, or one egg cup to see how it turns out. No matter what brand of air fryer you have sitting in your kitchen, here are some tips and hacks to help you succeed:

- **Add water to the bottom when cooking fatty foods:** Place ¼ to ½ cup (60 to 120 ml) of hot water in the bottom of the basket for an easier clean-up and to prevent the rendering fat from smoking. If your air fryer purges black smoke, whether through the vent or when you open the basket, stop the unit and unplug it, and do not use it until it is repaired.

- **Check for doneness:** Air fryers cook very quickly and use a lot of hot air, so food can overcook or dry out easily. One of the best parts about cooking with this unit is you can open the basket whenever you wish; just press pause and check your food. This will not affect the quality of the finished recipe.

- **Clean the air fryer after each use:** Wait for the basket to cool and clean it as directed (page 14). This will ensure the air fryer is ready to use whenever you need it, and it will continue to function efficiently.

- **Do not use wet batter:** Many deep-fried foods are dredged in wet batter, such as tempura vegetables, but this will not work in an air fryer. The wet batter just drips through and creates a mess. In this book, the battered items use a three-bowl system of flour, egg, and breadcrumbs to create light and flavorful breading. This dry breading is exceptional and crunchy when spritzed with a little oil and cooked in the air fryer.

- **Don't overcrowd:** Airflow around the food is one way this unit cooks quickly and efficiently; impeding the flow will produce poor results and uneven browning. Your food will steam instead of crisping. Arrange the food on the tray or in the basket with at least 1 inch (2.5 cm) between the pieces and a single layer where directed, and cook in batches whenever necessary. Items like fries and roasted vegetables can be piled as long as you toss them frequently.

- **Don't use aerosol sprays:** Store-bought oil sprays can damage the finish on the air fryer's interior components and reduce their life. If you must use this type of spray, only spray the food on areas that do not touch the basket and do not do this while the food is sitting in the unit.

- **Don't use dry seasoning:** Seasoning rubs can blow right off the products in the unit, so make sure you use pastes, or put the seasoning in sauces.

- **Flip, turn, or toss the food:** This ensures even cooking and browning.

- **Preheat the air fryer:** You will not have to do this for every recipe; I will direct preheating where appropriate for the recipes in this book. Preheating ensures the food starts cooking right away, and the recommended timing will be correct.

- **Prep any accessories:** Line the basket with perforated parchment or spray with oil whenever recommended. Prepare baking dishes, ramekins, and pizza pans with oil to ensure your food does not stick and these items will be easy to clean.

- **Secure bread on sandwiches:** The fan in an air fryer is strong enough to blow bread right off a sandwich if you don't pin it down with toothpicks. Just make sure you remove them before eating.

- **Use a manual timer:** This is my hack to ensure I turn my food at the right time, because I am compulsive after years in kitchens. If a food has to cook for 20 minutes, I set my timer for 10 minutes and the unit timer for 20. You do not have to do this, but then you do not have to watch the timer on the unit.

- **Use oil when necessary and apply it evenly:** Some foods do not need oil, such as casseroles, cakes, egg dishes, and pasta, but anything breaded, and pastry, will require a light coating. Even application means uniform browning, which looks nice, and the uncoated breading will be dry and unpalatable. Remember, do not use aerosol oil sprays in the air fryer, especially on the components or basket.

- **Use ventilation already in your kitchen:** Cook under vent hoods or near them and turn the fans on when cooking. Depending on what you are making, the unit will vent, so I like to whisk the steam and hot air away.

BEST OILS FOR AIR FRYING

Look around your kitchen and think about what oil is your favorite for cooking. You might have more than one for sweet or savory dishes. For example, olive oil isn't a great option for baked goods because the taste is too strong. In an air fryer, it is best to use an oil with a smoke point higher than 400°F (200°C), so the product can stand up to the high temperatures. Some oils to avoid are melted butter, coconut oil, and extra-virgin olive oil. Here are some oils that work well:

- **Avocado oil:** smoke point 520°F (270°C); great for baking and flavorless

- **Olive oil:** smoke point 460°F (235°C); for veggies or pizza

- **Peanut oil:** smoke point 450°F (230°C); flavorless, but obviously not appropriate for those with allergies

- **Safflower oil:** smoke point 510°F (265°C); flavorless

Care and Safety

If you already have an air fryer, you can probably just skim this section. Knowing the safety considerations and how to care for the unit are crucial for continuous use and effective operation. This appliance is not complicated, and maintenance takes minutes, even between batches and recipes. After unpacking the unit, the first step should be to read the manual and then keep it in a kitchen drawer or in the place where you store all the various instructions for appliances and other household items. All the information you need to know about safety and care is in the manual. But for a quick reference, here are some tips to keep your air fryer in top shape:

- Make sure the appliance is at least 5 inches (13 cm) away from other appliances and walls. The hot air should not vent near electrical outlets. And keep your hands and face away from the vents while the unit is running. Also, don't place anything on top of the air fryer.
- Unplug the air fryer when you are not using it.
- Place the unit on a heatproof surface when using it, because the bottom can get hot and might scorch your countertops. The sides and top can also be hot during and after use, so use silicone gloves or oven mitts if you need to touch it.
- Make sure your parchment liners and aluminum foil are secured with food or secured to the pan in the unit because the powerful fan can blow these items around. If the paper is blown against the heating element, it can burn.
- Don't use aerosol cooking sprays in the air fryer. This has been stated before but is worth another mention. These products can break down the coating on the basket and other components. To keep the finish pristine, do not salt your food directly in the unit, either, because salt can cause the interior surface finish to peel.
- Let the air fryer cool and unplug it before cleaning.
- Wipe the exterior with a damp cloth and don't spray cleaner directly on the unit because it can get inside the vents.
- Take the basket, trays, and racks out of the unit and let them cool completely before washing them with warm, soapy water. I usually place the basket in the sink and, after it is cool, fill it halfway with water, covering the racks and trays inside, letting them soak for 20 minutes.
- Do not use abrasive or corrosive cleaners or scouring cloths on any part of the air fryer.
- Use a brush to get any food and grease from between the holes in the basket insert. It is a nonstick surface, so clean-up will be easy.
- Store the air fryer with the cord tucked away on a flat surface after it is cool.
- If you have a toaster oven–style air fryer, line the trays with foil for easier clean-up.
- Bring the air fryer to an authorized service provider if you have any issues with it.

About the Recipes

Now that you are acquainted with your air fryer, let's take a look at the recipes. In this book, there are one hundred plant-based recipes to enjoy, from all over the world. You will find tantalizing spices, traditional dishes from every continent, and exotic flavor combinations in most chapters. This is not a reheating cookbook with lots of premade items or frozen convenience foods. You will be cooking from scratch, and it will be easy and quick in the air fryer. The recipes use whole ingredients for the most part, and the products can be found in your local grocery store, nothing too outlandish. The servings are designed for two to four people; air fryers are not meant to be used to prepare vast quantities of food. If you have a larger air fryer, the recipes can be doubled to reflect the larger area in the unit. You will find breakfasts, lunches, soups, sandwiches, appetizers, side dishes, main courses, desserts, and baked items in the following pages. Keep in mind that every air fryer is slightly different, so you might have to tweak the time and temperature for perfect results. Start with the recommended settings for each dish and adjust up or down. Have some fun; cooking is one of the most creative, pleasing activities you can undertake, especially when you can put delicious meals on the table for family and friends. So, let's get started!

TOOLS YOU WILL NEED FOR THESE RECIPES

You probably already have most, if not all, of the tools you need to make the recipes in this book in your kitchen already, so you will not have to go out and spend a lot of money. Here's what you'll need:

- 6- or 7-inch (15 or 18 cm) springform pan (or whatever size fits in your air fryer)
- 6- or 7- inch (15 or 18 cm) round baking dishes (or whatever size fits in your air fryer)
- Aluminum foil
- Box grater
- Cutting boards
- Electric hand beaters
- Food processor, immersion blender, or regular blender
- Knives
- Nested stainless-steel bowls
- Parchment paper
- Ramekins (4-ounce, 6-ounce)
- Saucepans
- Silicone muffin cups
- Skillets
- Stockpots
- Whisk, spoons, tongs

Breakfast

No matter your breakfast preference—sweet or savory—you will find a new favorite day-starter in these choices. My husband's go-to meal is now breakfast pizza, eaten as he rushes out the door at 5:00 a.m. I break the yolk on his pizza, so he can enjoy his meal without dripping all over his shirt. If you are not a breakfast person already, your air fryer makes it simple to start eating this important meal. Light choices such as crunchy granola–topped grapefruit and tasty egg muffins can be marvelous training-wheel choices for breakfast-averse people. Filling options, including creamy baked oatmeal and spicy huevos rancheros, will boost your energy all the way to lunch and beyond. Dive in, and breakfast could become your favorite meal of the day.

Romaine and Feta Frittata page 32

Grapefruit Granola Brûlée with Greek Yogurt

SERVES 2 ■ PREP TIME: 10 MINUTES, PLUS COOLING TIME ■ COOK TIME: 30 MINUTES

When my friends were tucking into sugary cocoa puffs, or whatever the popular cereal was at the time, my mother served us deep-hued ruby red grapefruit halves sprinkled with sugar. The combination of sweet and tart was intoxicating, and the color spectacular. I still eat peeled grapefruits as a snack to this day. Topping this pretty fruit with a layer of caramelized sugar and air fryer toasty granola is an absolute treat, and you will wonder why you never tried it before.

1 cup (156 g) rolled oats

¼ cup (28 g) chopped pecans

¼ cup (28 g) slivered almonds

2 tablespoons (18 g) sunflower seeds

2 tablespoons (18 g) pumpkin seeds

1 tablespoon (11 g) chia seeds

⅛ teaspoon ground cinnamon

Pinch sea salt

2 tablespoons (40 g) maple syrup

1 tablespoon (15 ml) canola oil

1 ruby red grapefruit, halved crosswise

2 tablespoons (30 g) brown sugar

¼ cup (60 g) vanilla Greek yogurt

1. Preheat the air fryer on Roast at 260°F (130°C) for 3 minutes.
2. Combine the oats, pecans, almonds, sunflower seeds, pumpkin seeds, chia seeds, cinnamon, and salt in a medium bowl. Add the maple syrup and oil and toss to coat.
3. Place the oat mixture in a 7-inch (18 cm) round baking pan and cook for 25 to 28 minutes, stirring every 7 minutes, until browned and crunchy. Spread the hot granola onto a parchment-lined baking sheet and let it cool to room temperature, about 45 minutes, stirring occasionally.
4. While the granola is cooling, place the grapefruit halves cut-side down on paper towels to soak up excess juice for at least 30 minutes.
5. Turn the halves cut-side up and use a paring knife to loosen the sections from the membranes, then sprinkle half the sugar on each half, spreading it out evenly. Use a kitchen torch to caramelize and melt the sugar (brûlée).
6. Top each half with ¼ to ⅓ cup (25 to 30 g) of granola and a dollop of yogurt.
7. Store the remaining granola in an airtight container for up to a week at room temperature.

Pear Pecan Breakfast Cake

SERVES 4 ■ PREP TIME: 10 MINUTES ■ COOK TIME: 35 MINUTES

A cake can be a perfectly acceptable breakfast choice, especially if packed with spices, chunks of ripe pear, and crunchy pecans. This lovely vanilla-infused creation bakes up moist and golden in your air fryer and will not heat up the kitchen during the warm temperatures of the summer. If you require a vegan version, swap the butter for a butter-flavored nondairy spread, the egg for a flax egg (see below), and the buttermilk for coconut or almond milk.

Butter, for greasing

¼ cup (55 g) unsalted butter, at room temperature

⅔ cup (120 g) granulated sugar

1 large egg

1 teaspoon vanilla extract

¾ cup (94 g) all-purpose flour, plus extra for dusting

½ teaspoon ground cinnamon

½ teaspoon baking powder

½ teaspoon baking soda

⅛ teaspoon sea salt

½ cup (120 ml) buttermilk

½ cup (75 g) chopped pear

½ cup (55 g) chopped pecans

1. Lightly butter a 7-inch (18 cm) round baking pan and dust it with flour.
2. In a medium bowl, cream the butter and sugar with electric handheld beaters until fluffy, scraping down the bowl's sides at least once, about 3 minutes.
3. Add the egg and vanilla and beat to combine.
4. In a medium bowl, stir the flour, cinnamon, baking powder, baking soda, and salt until mixed.
5. Add the flour mixture and buttermilk in three additions, starting and ending with the dry ingredients, beating after each addition and scraping down the bowl's sides.
6. Fold in the pear and pecans, then transfer the batter to the prepared pan.
7. Preheat the air fryer on Roast at 315°F (160°C) for 3 minutes.
8. Cook the cake for 30 to 35 minutes, or until golden brown and a toothpick inserted in the center of the cake comes out clean.
9. Cool the cake in the pan for 15 minutes, then turn it out onto a wire rack to cool completely before serving.

How to Make a Flax Egg

To replace an egg with a flax egg, mix 1 tablespoon flaxseed (7 g) with 3 tablespoons (45 ml) of water and let the mixture stand for 15 minutes to thicken.

Baked Steel-Cut Oatmeal with Mixed Fruit

SERVES 4 ■ PREP TIME: 10 MINUTES ■ COOK TIME: 30 MINUTES

Oatmeal is the epitome of comfort food, the original stick-to-the-ribs dish eaten as a budget-friendly, filling breakfast by generations of people. In an air fryer, oatmeal becomes a convenient one-pot meal with no extra dishes to wash or slaving over the stove required. The fruit topping adds sweetness and a healthy hit of fiber and antioxidants, but baked oatmeal is equally delicious with a splash of milk and an extra drizzle of maple syrup.

1 cup (235 ml) whole milk or your favorite dairy-free milk

1 large egg

½ cup (78 g) steel-cut oats

2 tablespoons (40 g) maple syrup

⅛ teaspoon ground nutmeg

Dash sea salt

1 cup (150 g) mixed chopped fruit (strawberries, peaches, blueberries, raspberries, bananas)

1. Preheat the air fryer on Roast at 340°F (175°C) for 3 minutes.
2. In a 7-inch (18 cm) round baking pan, mix the milk, egg, oats, maple syrup, nutmeg, and salt until well blended. Stir in the fruit and cover tightly with aluminum foil.
3. Cook for 30 minutes, stirring halfway through, or until the liquid is absorbed and the oats are tender. Serve hot.

French Toast Sticks with Cinnamon Mascarpone Sauce

SERVES 2 ■ PREP TIME: 10 MINUTES ■ COOK TIME: 15 MINUTES

If given a choice of any breakfast in the world, my choice would be golden French toast, either dipped in this delectable, cinnamon-spiked sauce or topped with pure maple syrup. I can now whip up a batch with no fuss or mess in my air fryer, in minutes. The trick to getting the best results in this recipe is to make sure you shake off the excess soaking mixture, or the bread will be uneven in color and vaguely eggy. Add a little orange zest for a lovely citrus variation.

French Toast Sticks

½ cup (120 ml) whole milk

2 large eggs

1 tablespoon (15 g) brown sugar

1 teaspoon vanilla extract

Pinch sea salt

4 thick slices bread (such as brioche, Texas toast, French bread), cut into thirds

Oil spray

Cinnamon Mascarpone Sauce

1 cup (240 g) mascarpone, at room temperature

¼ cup (80 g) maple syrup

1 teaspoon vanilla extract

½ teaspoon ground cinnamon

Pinch ground cloves

1. In a medium bowl, whisk together the milk, eggs, brown sugar, vanilla, and salt until very well blended.
2. Preheat on Air Fry at 375°F (190°C) for 3 minutes. Lightly oil a 7-inch (18 cm) round baking pan.
3. Add half the bread sticks to the egg mixture, turning to coat.
4. Shake the excess egg mixture off the sticks and place them in a single layer in the pan. Spray lightly with oil and cook the sticks for 4 minutes. Turn them, spray lightly with oil, and cook for 2 to 3 minutes, or until golden brown.
5. Transfer the French toast sticks to a plate, loosely tent with foil to keep them warm, and repeat with the remaining bread sticks.
6. In a medium bowl, whisk the mascarpone, maple syrup, vanilla, cinnamon, and cloves until well mixed. Spoon the sauce into 2 small bowls and serve with warm French toast sticks.
7. Refrigerate leftover sauce in a covered container for up to 5 days.

Applesauce Donut Holes

MAKES 12 ■ PREP TIME: 15 MINUTES ■ COOK TIME: 20 MINUTES

Sometimes nothing is better than warm, spiced donuts for breakfast, so the fact you can make them at home in less than thirty minutes is awesome. These donut holes are not overly sweet, so the light sugar glaze added before cooking creates the perfect taste. You have to roll the donuts in the sugar before air frying because the finished donuts are too dry for the sugar to stick, unlike deep-frying, where the oil creates the base for the sugar.

2 cups (250 g) all-purpose flour

⅓ cup (75 g) brown sugar

1¼ teaspoon baking powder

½ teaspoon ground cinnamon

¼ teaspoon ground nutmeg

¼ teaspoon baking soda

¼ teaspoon salt

Pinch ground cloves

¾ cup (180 g) unsweetened applesauce

3 tablespoons (45 g) melted butter

3 tablespoons (45 g) whole milk

1 large egg, beaten

1 teaspoon vanilla extract

½ cup (100 g) granulated sugar

½ teaspoon ground cinnamon

Oil spray

1. In a large bowl, stir together the flour, brown sugar, baking powder, cinnamon, nutmeg, baking soda, salt, and cloves until blended.
2. In a medium bowl, beat together the applesauce, butter, milk, egg, and vanilla with electric handheld beaters until combined.
3. Add the wet ingredients to the dry and stir until a soft dough is formed, thick enough to roll into balls.
4. In a small bowl, stir together the sugar and cinnamon.
5. Using a tablespoon, scoop the batter and drop it into the sugar mixture. Roll the batter in the sugar, forming it into a small ball, about 18 times in total.
6. Preheat on Air Fry at 360°F (185°C) for 3 minutes.
7. Cut a piece of parchment paper so it fits the air fryer basket with 1 inch (2.5 cm) all around the sides for airflow. Place the parchment in the basket and lightly coat with cooking spray.
8. Place half the donut holes in the basket in a single layer (don't overcrowd), and cook for 8 to 10 minutes, turning halfway through, until cooked through and crispy.
9. Repeat with the remaining donut holes and serve.

Goat Cheese Breakfast Pizzas

SERVES 2 ■ PREP TIME: 15 MINUTES ■ COOK TIME: 22 MINUTES

As a teenager, I ordered a pizza in a sidewalk café in Malta, thinking I would get standard fare, especially since I was so close to Italy. Much to my horror, my pizza arrived with a fried egg baked right into one-quarter of the crust. It turned out to be delicious and became the inspiration for this interesting breakfast dish. The air fryer produces spectacular pizza with a gorgeous, crispy crust, melted cheese, and perfectly cooked eggs. When you cut into the pizza, the rich yolk spills over the tangy goat cheese and vegetables. Delicious!

12 ounces (340 g) premade pizza dough

2 teaspoons olive oil, divided, plus extra for brushing

4 ounces (113 g) crumbled goat cheese, divided

1 medium tomato, chopped, divided

2 large eggs, divided

Sea salt

Freshly ground black pepper

1 cup (30 g) shredded baby spinach, divided

1. Divide the pizza dough into 2 equal pieces and roll them out into 7-inch (18 cm) circles.
2. Preheat on Air Fry at 375°F (190°C) for 3 minutes.
3. Brush the air fryer basket with oil, place a pizza dough onto the wire trivet in the basket, and pierce it all over with a fork. Brush the dough lightly with half the oil and cook for 3 minutes.
4. Take the crust out and turn it over so the browned side is on the bottom. Crumble half the goat cheese on the pizza to the edges and top with half the tomato. Crack an egg onto the pizza near the center, spreading the white out a little. Season the whole pizza with salt and pepper and cook until the egg whites are set and yolks a little runny, about 8 minutes.
5. Repeat with the remaining ingredients and serve the pizzas topped with the spinach.

Creamy Thyme Mushrooms on Toast

SERVES 2 ■ PREP TIME: 10 MINUTES ■ COOK TIME: 10 MINUTES

One of my favorite positions as a chef introduced me to this deceptively simple, mouth-wateringly delicious dish—the most popular appetizer on the menu. Mushrooms become sweeter when caramelized, and with the air fryer, there is no supervision required. If possible, use an assortment of wild mushrooms for an exotic flavor, such as shiitake, morel, oyster, portobello, and enoki. One of the benefits of eating this recipe as breakfast is research linking a mushroom-rich breakfast to consuming fewer calories later in the day because mushrooms create a feeling of fullness and less hunger.[1]

3 cups (210 g) quartered mushrooms

2 teaspoons olive oil

½ teaspoon garlic powder

¼ cup (60 ml) heavy (whipping) cream

2 tablespoons (30 g) cream cheese, at room temperature

1 tablespoon (11 g) grainy mustard

Sea salt

Freshly ground black pepper

2 thick slices sourdough or French bread, toasted

2 teaspoons chopped parsley

1. Toss the mushrooms, oil, and garlic powder in a medium bowl.
2. Preheat on Air Fry at 380°F (195°C) for 3 minutes.
3. Spread the mushrooms in the air fryer basket and cook until lightly caramelized and tender, about 10 minutes, stirring halfway through.
4. While the mushrooms are cooking, in a medium bowl, whisk the cream, cream cheese, and mustard until smooth and season with salt and pepper.
5. Add the mushrooms and any juice in the bottom of the air fryer to the creamy sauce and stir to combine.
6. Serve the mushrooms on the toasted bread and top with parsley.

---

1 Hess Julie M., Qi Wang, Clarissa Kraft, and Joanne L Slavin. "Impact of Agaricus bisporus mushroom consumption on satiety and food intake." *Appetite* vol. 117 (2017): 179 –185. doi:10.1016/j.appet.2017.06.021

Basil Pesto Baked Eggs

SERVES 2 ■ PREP TIME: 10 MINUTES ■ COOK TIME: 10 MINUTES

Sunny yellow yolks, bright white goat cheese, and lovely, deep dark greens make this a stunning dish. As the air fryer works its magic, the spinach wilts and forms a tasty cradle for the eggs; all you need to do is scoop out a portion and enjoy. Try this nutrient-packed recipe with Crispy Latkes with Sour Cream and Apple (page 28) for a full breakfast.

3 cups (90 g) chopped spinach

¼ cup (65 g) basil pesto

¼ cup (60 ml) heavy (whipping) cream

¼ cup (37 g) crumbled goat cheese

4 large eggs

1. In a large bowl, toss together the spinach, pesto, and cream until well mixed.
2. Spread the spinach mixture in a 7-inch (18 cm) round baking pan and sprinkle with the cheese. Make 4 wells in the mixture with the back of a spoon and carefully crack an egg into each well. (You may wish to crack each egg into a small bowl before pouring into the wells.)
3. Preheat on Air Fry at 330°F (170°C) for 3 minutes.
4. Cook until the egg whites are set, and the greens are wilted, about 10 minutes. Serve.

Crispy Latkes with Sour Cream and Apple

SERVES 4 ■ PREP TIME: 15 MINUTES ■ COOK TIME: 45 MINUTES

Latkes—a traditional Jewish dish— are potato pancakes made from shredded potato, onion, and garlic fried into a crispy, golden lattice, the ideal base for tender butter-sautéed apples. As an eight- or nine-year-old, I watched my beautiful Oma prepare latkes from a family recipe and burned my fingers and tongue because I couldn't wait to eat them. The air fryer creates the same texture and lovely color with very little oil and less time, but they still are very hot coming out, so don't scorch your fingers!

3 large russet potatoes, scrubbed and grated

½ small sweet onion, grated

2 tablespoons (14 g) breadcrumbs

1 tablespoon (8 g) cornstarch

1 large egg

¼ teaspoon garlic powder

Sea salt

Freshly ground black pepper

Oil spray

1 tablespoon (14 g) butter

2 apples, peeled and thinly sliced

⅛ teaspoon ground cinnamon

½ cup (115 g) sour cream

1. Place the grated potato and onion in the center of a clean kitchen cloth, fold up the sides to form a pouch, and twist, holding the ends of the pouch, to squeeze out as much liquid as possible.
2. Place the dry potato and onion in a large bowl and stir in the breadcrumbs, cornstarch, egg, and garlic powder until very well mixed. Season with salt and pepper and let the mixture stand for 10 minutes.
3. Preheat on Air Fry at 360°F (185°C) for 3 minutes.
4. Spray the air fryer basket with oil. Working in batches, scoop out ¼-cup (30 g) measures of the potato mixture and form them into 3-inch (7 cm) patties. Place them in the basket in a single layer, about 4 per batch, and cook for 8 to 10 minutes, turning halfway through, until golden and crispy.
5. Transfer the cooked latkes to a plate and repeat with the remaining potato mixture.
6. While you are cooking the last batch, melt the butter in a small skillet over medium-high heat. Sauté the apples and cinnamon until tender and lightly browned, about 5 minutes. Set aside.
7. Serve the latkes warm with the apple and a dollop of sour cream. (Make sure you check the nutrition label on the sour cream—some brands contain rennet or gelatin, which are animal products.)

Spicy Tofu Huevos Rancheros

SERVES 4 ■ PREP TIME: 15 MINUTES, PLUS PRESSING AND MARINATING TIME ■ COOK TIME: 30 MINUTES

Tofu scramble is a staple in the vegan world because you do not notice the lack of eggs when it is prepared correctly. This version features crisp tofu cubes, cooked to a perfect golden turn in the air fryer rather than a skillet. The added texture and smoky flavor combine beautifully with traditional huevos rancheros fillings such as creamy avocado and fresh, vibrant salsa.

1 (14-ounce/400 g) block extra-firm tofu

1 tablespoon (15 ml) olive oil

½ teaspoon ground cumin

½ teaspoon garlic powder

¼ teaspoon onion powder

¼ teaspoon paprika

⅛ teaspoon sea salt

Oil spray

4 (8-inch/20 cm) corn or flour tortillas

½ cup (60 g) shredded cheddar cheese

½ cup (130 g) tomato salsa, homemade or store-bought

½ avocado, chopped

1 tablespoon (1 g) chopped fresh cilantro

Optional toppings

Sour cream

Pickled onions

Black beans

Lime wedges

1. Wrap the tofu block in a clean kitchen cloth and put it on a plate. Place another plate on top and weigh it down with a large 28-ounce (800 g) can. Let the tofu stand for at least 30 minutes, unwrap, and cut into ½-inch (1 cm) cubes.
2. In a medium bowl, stir together the olive oil, cumin, garlic powder, onion powder, paprika, and salt until blended. Add the tofu, toss to coat, cover, and marinate in the refrigerator at least 30 minutes or up to 3 hours.
3. Preheat on Air Fry at 375°F (190°C) for 3 minutes. Lightly spray the air fryer basket with oil.
4. Working in batches, place the tofu in the basket, taking care not to overcrowd, spray lightly with oil, and cook for 14 minutes, shaking every 5 minutes, until lightly browned and warmed through. Set the cooked tofu aside on a plate covered lightly with foil and repeat with the remaining tofu.
5. In the last few minutes of cooking, wrap the tortillas in a clean kitchen cloth and warm in the microwave for 30 seconds to 1 minute.
6. Spread the tortillas out on a clean work surface and evenly divide the tofu among them. Top with the salsa, cheese, avocado, and cilantro, and any other optional toppings.
7. Fold the sides of the tortillas over the filling and roll them up from the bottom, then serve.

Romaine and Feta Frittata

SERVES 4 ■ PREP TIME: 10 MINUTES ■ COOK TIME: 20 MINUTES

Cooked lettuce? Yes, robust lettuce like romaine, escarole, and endive are fabulous grilled, roasted, sautéed, or cooked into a creamy frittata with heaps of herbs and salty feta cheese. The taste of romaine becomes deeper and more complex, and the texture remains a little crisp. Sour cream adds an intriguing tanginess and creates a pleasing creaminess. A frittata is essentially a baked omelet, with the other ingredients baked right into the egg rather than the cooked egg folded over it. Making this frittata in an air fryer cuts the cooking time, so this tasty dish can become a regular meal even on a busy weekday.

Olive oil, for greasing

2 tablespoons (28 g) butter

2 cups (110 g) shredded romaine lettuce or Swiss chard

½ small sweet onion, chopped

6 large eggs

¼ cup (60 ml) whole milk

¼ cup (60 g) sour cream

2 tablespoons (5 g) chopped mixed fresh herbs (such as basil, thyme, oregano)

Sea salt

Freshly ground black pepper

½ cup (75 g) crumbled feta cheese

1. Grease a 7-inch (18 cm) round baking pan with olive oil.
2. Melt the butter in a large skillet over medium-high heat and sauté the lettuce and onion until softened, 5 to 6 minutes. Transfer the greens to the baking pan.
3. In a medium bowl, whisk the eggs, milk, sour cream, and herbs and season with salt and pepper. Pour the eggs over the greens, stirring slightly to distribute them throughout the eggs. Top with the feta cheese.
4. Preheat on Air Fry at 350°F (180°C) for 3 minutes.
5. Cook the frittata until the eggs are cooked through and light brown, about 15 minutes. Serve.

Tuscan Eggs with Sundried Tomato

SERVES 2 ■ PREP TIME: 10 MINUTES ■ COOK TIME: 40 MINUTES

This is my own spin on shakshuka, a dish I enjoyed when I worked in North Africa as a chef. This version includes sweet sundried tomatoes, basil, and Parmesan cheese as a nod to Italy, a region famous for its produce and complex tomato-based sauces. If you enjoy a little heat with your eggs, add half a chile pepper or a generous pinch of red pepper flakes to the sauce.

1 leek, sliced and washed thoroughly

½ red onion, sliced

1 red bell pepper, chopped

1 green zucchini, diced

1 tablespoon (15 g) olive oil

1 teaspoon minced garlic

1 (15-ounce/425 g) can diced tomatoes

¼ cup (14 g) sliced sundried tomatoes

1 tablespoon (2.5 g) chopped fresh basil

2 large eggs

¼ cup (25 g) Parmesan cheese

1. In a large bowl, toss the leek, onion, bell pepper, zucchini, oil, and garlic until well coated.
2. Preheat on Air Fry at 380°F (195°C) for 3 minutes.
3. Place the vegetables in the air fryer basket and cook until tender, about 10 minutes.
4. While the vegetables are cooking, heat the tomatoes in a small skillet over medium-high heat until simmering.
5. Transfer the vegetables and any juice in the bottom of the basket to a 7-inch (18 cm) round baking pan (3-inches/7.5 cm deep) and stir in the tomatoes and basil. Cook for 12 to 15 minutes, stirring halfway through, until the mixture is very hot.
6. Reduce the heat to 340°F (175°C) and make 2 wide wells in the tomato mixture with the back of a spoon. Crack an egg into a small bowl and transfer it to a well, then repeat. Cook until the egg whites are set, about 8 minutes.
7. Serve topped with Parmesan cheese.

PHILIPS
TurboStar technology
350 °F
0 min

Bulgur Egg Muffins

SERVES 3 ■ PREP TIME: 10 MINUTES ■ COOK TIME: 12 MINUTES

Grab-and-go food is a popular alternative to a sit-down meal in this hectic, over-scheduled world. If that convenient option is nutritious and appetizing, even better. Egg muffins are a staple for most air fryer enthusiasts because they cook up perfectly every time, and the range of added ingredients is endless. This recipe boosts iron content with nutty bulgur and creamy goat cheese. Try slicing a couple egg muffins and wrapping them in a tortilla with shredded lettuce and a teaspoon of pesto for an easy Mediterranean-style wrap.

Olive oil, for greasing

1 cup (185 g) cooked bulgur

3 large eggs

¼ cup (37 g) crumbled goat cheese

¼ cup (14 g) chopped or slivered sundried tomatoes

2 tablespoons (6 g) chopped black olives

1 tablespoon (2.5 g) chopped fresh oregano

Sea salt

Freshly ground black pepper

1. Lightly grease 6 silicone muffin cups or ramekins.
2. Preheat on Air Fry at 300°F (150°C) for 3 minutes.
3. In a large bowl, mix together the bulgur, eggs, goat cheese, sundried tomatoes, olives, and oregano. Season with salt and pepper. Transfer the mixture to the muffin cups.
4. Cook for 10 to 12 minutes, until lightly golden and set. Serve.

Freeze the egg muffins individually in sealed plastic bags for up to 2 months. When you want one as a snack or for breakfast, take the muffin out and let it thaw in the refrigerator overnight or microwave for 1 minute.

Coddled Herb Eggs

SERVES 3 ■ PREP TIME: 10 MINUTES ■ COOK TIME: 8 MINUTES

These aren't technically coddled eggs, which are made in a coddler and have a luscious cream topping, but that name is my Nana's for this dish, so I am going with it. The added cream prevents the whites from having a dreaded rubbery texture, so take the time to swirl it in. These eggs can be the topping for a California eggs benedict (toasted English muffin and sliced avocado) or can be spooned over a crispy potato or root vegetable hash.

Butter, for greasing

3 large eggs

Sea salt

Freshly ground black pepper

3 tablespoons (45 ml) heavy cream

1 tablespoon (2.5 g) chopped parsley

1. Preheat on Air Fry at 300°F (150°C) for 3 minutes.
2. Grease 3 (4-ounce/120 ml) ramekins or silicone cups with butter.
3. Break 1 egg into each ramekin. Season the eggs lightly with salt and pepper and spoon 1 table-spoon (15 ml) of cream into each egg white, swirling it gently without breaking the yolks.
4. Cook until the egg whites are set, about 8 minutes. Check after 6 minutes to see if the eggs are at the doneness you prefer.
5. Serve topped with the parsley.

Soups and Sandwiches

When you work for decades as a chef, one of the main conversations between colleagues is what kind of restaurant we would open if the planets aligned and money was no object. Amidst the trendy fusion and extreme fine-dining choices sat my very humble soup-and-sandwich bistro dreams. I love soup and would make it every day if my family wouldn't stage an intervention. And what is soup without a sandwich to dip in it? The recipes in this chapter are a few of my favorites, ones I make weekly depending on produce availability. The soups are made with vegetables roasted to tender perfection in the air fryer and then puréed with the other ingredients to create luscious combinations. The sandwiches are not delicate creations; they require both hands and, in some cases, a stack of napkins. Serve them together to special guests for dinner and watch every drop and crumb disappear.

Golden Apple Brie Sandwich page 46

Roasted Red Pepper Tomato Soup

SERVES 4 ■ PREP TIME: 15 MINUTES ■ COOK TIME: 25 MINUTES

Red bell peppers and tomatoes become sweet and smoky when roasted, either in the oven or, in this case, an air fryer. The rich taste is deepened even further with the addition of garlic and balsamic vinegar. You can certainly substitute yellow or orange bell peppers instead, but the color will not be a luscious red. If you happen to have leftovers (unlikely!), serve them spooned over pasta with a generous sprinkle of Parmesan and fresh basil.

1½ pounds (680 g) tomatoes, quartered

1 red bell pepper, quartered

2 celery stalks, cut into 1-inch (2 cm) pieces

½ sweet onion, cut into 1-inch (2 cm) pieces

3 garlic cloves, smashed

2 tablespoons (30 ml) olive oil

2 tablespoons (60 ml) balsamic vinegar

2 cups (475 ml) low-sodium vegetable broth

½ cup (120 ml) coconut cream or heavy (whipping) cream

2 tablespoons (5 g) chopped fresh basil

Sea salt

Freshly ground black pepper

1. In a medium bowl, toss the tomatoes, bell pepper, celery, onion, garlic, oil, and vinegar until well mixed.
2. Transfer the vegetables to the air fryer basket and Air Fry at 375°F (190°C) for 15 minutes, tossing halfway through, until tender and lightly charred.
3. In a food processor or blender, purée the vegetables and any liquid in the bottom of the air fryer with the broth until smooth.
4. Transfer the soup to a large saucepan and bring to a simmer over medium heat, about 5 minutes. Whisk in the cream and basil and season with salt and pepper. Serve.

Puréeing hot soup in a blender requires a few safety guidelines to avoid burning yourself. Remove the plug in the blender lid and use a thick kitchen cloth to hold the lid and cover the hole. This will let the steam escape, so the soup won't explode. Also, work in small batches, so the amount does not pulse up too high when blending.

Coconut Roasted Root Vegetable Soup

SERVES 4 ■ PREP TIME: 15 MINUTES ■ COOK TIME: 35 MINUTES

This is not a precise soup; inspiration can come from what you have in your refrigerator, from what you find at the store, or even from the bounty in your garden. The starchy root vegetables are sublime in the air fryer, tender and lightly browned in very little time. Try to find smaller parsnips about an inch (2.5 cm) in diameter—the large ones can be woody and slightly acrid. If you purchase the parsnips from a grocery store rather than growing them, make sure you peel or scrub them well because many growers apply a wax layer to protect the vegetables during shipping.

2 parsnips, peeled and cut into 1-inch (2 cm) pieces

1 sweet potato, peeled and cut into 1-inch (2 cm) pieces

1 potato, peeled and cut into 1-inch (2 cm) pieces

1 carrot, peeled and cut into 1-inch (2 cm) pieces

½ sweet onion, chopped

1 teaspoon minced garlic

1 tablespoon (15 ml) olive oil

3 cups (705 ml) vegetable broth

1 cup (235 ml) canned coconut milk

1 teaspoon ground cumin

½ teaspoon ground coriander

Sea salt

Freshly ground black pepper

1. In a large bowl, toss the parsnip, sweet potato, potato, carrot, onion, garlic, and oil until well coated.
2. Place the vegetables in the air fryer basket and Air Fry at 375°F (190°C) for 20 to 25 minutes, shaking once or twice, until very tender and lightly caramelized.
3. While the vegetables are cooking, bring the broth and coconut milk to a boil in a large saucepan over medium-high heat.
4. Working in batches, if needed, transfer the vegetables to a food processor, including any liquid in the bottom of the air fryer, and add half the broth mixture. Process until the soup is very smooth, adding more broth if needed.
5. Add the puréed vegetables to the saucepan, whisking to blend with the remaining broth. Add the cumin and coriander and season to taste with salt and pepper.
6. Bring to a simmer, then serve.

Fennel Celeriac Soup with Gremolata

SERVES 4 ■ PREP TIME: 15 MINUTES ■ COOK TIME: 35 MINUTES

You will love the exciting flavor combination of the vegetables in this coconut cream–accented soup, and the pretty parsley-based topping has interesting garlic and citrus accents. The bulk of the soup is made in the air fryer, but you will have to utilize a blender and finish this dish in a pot on the stove. If you have extra gremolata, it is delicious drizzled over asparagus or green beans, or as a topping for a hearty veggie stew.

Fennel Celeriac Soup

1 large fennel bulb, cut into 1-inch (2 cm) slices

1 small celeriac root, peeled and cut into 1-inch (2 cm) pieces

½ small sweet onion, cut into 1-inch (2 cm) pieces

1 tablespoon (15 ml) olive oil

Sea salt

Freshly ground black pepper

4 cups (950 ml) low-sodium vegetable broth

½ cup (120 ml) coconut cream

Gremolata

1 cup (60 g) chopped fresh parsley

1 teaspoon minced garlic

Juice and zest of ½ lemon

2 tablespoons (30 ml) olive oil

Sea salt

Freshly ground black pepper

1. In a large bowl, toss the fennel, celeriac, onion, and oil until well coated and season with salt and pepper.
2. Place the vegetables in the air fryer basket and Air Fry at 375°F (190°C) for 20 to 25 minutes, shaking once or twice, until very tender and lightly caramelized.
3. While the vegetables are cooking, make the gremolata by mixing the parsley, garlic, lemon juice, lemon zest, and oil together in a small bowl. Season with salt and pepper and set aside.
4. Working in batches if needed, transfer the vegetables to a food processor, including any liquid in the bottom of the air fryer, and add the broth. Process until the soup is very smooth, adding more broth if needed.
5. Transfer the soup to the large saucepan and add the coconut cream, whisking to blend. Bring to a simmer over medium heat and serve topped with the gremolata.

Baba Ghanoush Soup

SERVES 2 TO 4 ■ PREP TIME: 10 MINUTES ■ COOK TIME: 40 MINUTES

Baba Ghanoush is usually a tempting appetizer, but the flavor and texture combination works beautifully in a soup. Using an air fryer to cook the eggplant is incredibly easy; just choose a vegetable that fits the basket. You don't even have to cut it! This porous, slightly bitter vegetable soaks up any flavor added to it, such as the nutty tahini, warm spices, and fresh lemon juice in this dish. If you require a vegan meal, use canned coconut milk instead of heavy cream; its mild sweetness will enhance the already delightful taste.

1 large eggplant

1 tablespoon (15 ml) olive oil, divided

1 small sweet onion, diced

1 teaspoon minced garlic

½ teaspoon ground cumin

½ teaspoon ground coriander

3 cups (705 ml) low-sodium vegetable broth

¼ cup (60 ml) heavy (whipping) cream

2 tablespoons (30 g) tahini

Juice of ½ lemon

Sea salt

Freshly ground black pepper

1. Preheat on Air Fry at 390°F (195°C) for 3 minutes.
2. Rub the eggplant all over with 1 teaspoon of oil and place it in the air fryer basket. Cook for 20 to 25 minutes until very tender.
3. Remove the eggplant from the basket, place it in a medium bowl, cover the bowl tightly with plastic wrap, and let it steam for 15 minutes.
4. While the eggplant is steaming, heat the remaining oil in a large saucepan over medium-high heat. Sauté the onion and garlic until softened, about 5 minutes.
5. Add the cumin and coriander and sauté 1 minute. Add the vegetable broth, cream, tahini, and lemon juice and bring it to a simmer.
6. Peel the eggplant over the bowl, discarding the peels, and mash the flesh with any accumulated juices.
7. Add the eggplant flesh and juices and purée the soup in a food processor (or using a handheld immersion blender).
8. Transfer the puréed soup back to the saucepan and season with salt and pepper. Serve.

Roasted Beet Soup

SERVES 4 ■ PREP TIME: 10 MINUTES ■ COOK TIME: 25 MINUTES

Beets are often left in the grocery store's display case because many people do not know how to prepare them. This recipe is the perfect place to experiment with this glorious vegetable: roasting the beets highlights all their best characteristics, such as the luscious magenta color and earthy taste. Look for beets with their greens still attached, so you get two ingredients for the price of one. The beets can be popped into the air fryer for this delectable soup, and the greens tossed in a lovely accompanying salad.

10 medium beets, peeled and cut into ½-inch (1 cm) pieces

½ small sweet onion, peeled and cut into ½-inch (1 cm) pieces

2 garlic cloves, peeled and crushed

1 teaspoon olive oil

4 cups (950 ml) low-sodium vegetable broth

Juice of ½ lemon

Sea salt

Freshly ground black pepper

½ cup (115 g) sour cream

2 tablespoons (5 g) chopped fresh dill

1. In a medium bowl, toss the beets, onion, garlic, and olive oil until well coated.
2. Place the vegetables in the air fryer basket and Air Fry at 375°F (190°C) for 20 to 25 minutes, shaking once or twice, until very tender and lightly caramelized.
3. While the vegetables are cooking, bring the broth to a boil in a medium saucepan over medium-high heat. Reduce the heat to keep the broth simmering gently until the vegetables are finished.
4. Transfer the vegetables to a food processor, including any juices in the bottom of the air fryer, and add the broth. Process until the soup is very smooth, adding more broth if the soup is too thick.
5. Season with salt and pepper and serve topped with sour cream and dill.

How to Create Vegan Recipes from Vegetarian

Most of the recipes in this book are vegetarian, but many can be converted to vegan with a few quick substitutions. Milk can be replaced with nondairy milk, cream with coconut cream, sour cream or yogurt with a nondairy option, and in some cases, cheese with a vegan product. If you follow a vegan diet, you know which cheeses melt well (and some do not), so you can swap those in for recipes such as casseroles, or recipes in which the cheese is not cooked. The baking recipes should not be altered—if they are, expect a change in the texture or results.

Golden Apple Brie Sandwich

SERVES 2 ■ PREP TIME: 10 MINUTES ■ COOK TIME: 10 MINUTES

The area where I lived in Southern Ontario is bursting with incredible artisan and organic ingredients. One of my favorite people in the world, an exceptional British chef named Stephen, spearheaded a field-to-fork movement that brought us ripe, glossy apples, homemade jelly created from plump chile peppers, and creamy brie. I baked the fragrant golden bread, and between lunch and dinner service, the kitchen staff made these incredible sandwiches. It is quicker in the air fryer, and with every bite, I remember those talented chefs who taught me so much.

4 thick slices bread (sourdough or multigrain)

2 tablespoons (40 g) hot pepper jelly

1 (8-ounce/225 g) round brie, cut into ¼-inch (½ cm)-thick slices

½ tart apple, thinly sliced

2 tablespoons (28 g) butter, at room temperature

1. Place the bread slices on a clean work surface and spread them with the hot pepper jelly. Place brie slices on 2 pieces of bread and top with the apple slices. Evenly divide the remaining brie between the sandwiches and top with the other bread slices.
2. Preheat on Air Fry at 375°F (190°C) for 3 minutes.
3. Spread the butter evenly on the top of the sandwiches and place them butter-side down in the air fryer basket. Butter the remaining side and secure the sandwiches with toothpicks.
4. Cook for 8 to 10 minutes, flipping halfway through, until golden and the cheese is melted. Remove the toothpicks and serve.

Barbecue Tofu and Mango Sandwich

SERVES 2 ■ PREP TIME: 15 MINUTES ■ COOK TIME: 35 MINUTES

If you crave the taste of barbecue, this sandwich will prove meat is not necessary to enjoy smoky, bold flavors. In the air fryer, the tofu crisps on the edges similar to grilling, and the even heat finishes the sauce to a tempting, sticky glaze. The sandwich can be served without the chutney, but the ginger and jalapeño-infused mango mixture elevates the flavor to new culinary heights. Choose ripe mangos with a perceptible fragrance through the skin; this ensures the flesh will be a vibrant yellow and the taste sweet and piney.

Mango Chutney

1 teaspoon avocado or olive oil

¼ red bell pepper, diced

¼ sweet onion, diced

1 tablespoon (10 g) minced jalapeño pepper

½ teaspoon peeled and grated fresh ginger

1 large mango, chopped

Juice and zest of ½ lime

1 teaspoon chopped fresh cilantro

Sea salt

Freshly ground black pepper

Barbecue Tofu Sandwiches

1 (14-ounce/400 g) block extra-firm tofu, pressed (see page 30) and cut into ¼-inch (½ cm) thick slices

1 cup (250 g) barbecue sauce, homemade or store-bought

Avocado oil, for brushing

2 crusty buns, halved lengthwise and toasted (optional)

2 cups (40 g) arugula or baby spinach

1. Heat the oil in a medium saucepan over medium-high heat. Sauté the bell pepper, onion, jalapeño pepper, and ginger until softened, about 3 minutes.

2. Add the mango, lime juice, and lime zest and sauté until the mixture is heated through, about 3 minutes.

(continued)

(continued)

3. Remove from the heat, stir in the cilantro, and season with salt and pepper. Transfer the chutney to a container, partially cover, and chill. Store in the refrigerator until you are ready to use it, up to 5 days.
4. On a large plate, coat the tofu slices with barbecue sauce on all sides.
5. Preheat on Air Fry at 360°F (185°C) for 3 minutes.
6. Brush the air fryer basket with oil and arrange half the tofu slices in a single layer. Cook 15 minutes until glazed and lightly caramelized on the edges, turning halfway through and shaking the basket several times. Repeat with the remaining tofu.
7. Pile the barbecued tofu on the buns and top with a generous scoop of the mango chutney and the arugula. Serve.

Summer Vegetable Sandwich with Feta

SERVES 4 ■ PREP TIME: 15 MINUTES ■ COOK TIME: 12 MINUTES

Make sure you have a thick stack of napkins when you tuck into these hearty, two-hander sandwiches. They are not meant for the faint of heart! The Mediterranean-inspired ingredients are the perfect balance of sweet, salty, and tart. The layers of perfectly roasted vegetables, snowy feta cheese, and fresh basil look gorgeous enough to serve to company. Look for an aged balsamic vinegar rather than a generic brand because the taste is complex and less astringent—or try a white balsamic.

1 baby eggplant, halved lengthwise and cut into ¼-inch (½ cm) slices

1 zucchini, cut into ¼-inch (½ cm) slices

1 red bell pepper, cut into ¼-inch (½ cm) slices

½ red onion, cut into ¼-inch (½ cm) slices

1 tablespoon olive oil

1 tablespoon balsamic vinegar

Sea salt

Freshly ground black pepper

1 baguette, halved lengthwise and widthwise into 4 pieces, toasted (optional)

¼ cup sliced oil-packed sundried tomatoes

½ cup crumbled feta cheese

2 tablespoons chopped fresh basil

1. Preheat on Air Fry at 375°F (190°C) for 3 minutes.
2. In a large bowl, toss the eggplant, zucchini, bell pepper, onion, oil, and balsamic vinegar until the vegetables are coated. Season lightly with salt and pepper.
3. Transfer the vegetables to the air fryer basket. Cook for 10 to 12 minutes, tossing once or twice, until tender and lightly caramelized.
4. Evenly divide the vegetables between the pieces of bread and top with sundried tomatoes, feta, and basil. Serve.

Philly Cheese Portobello Mushroom Sandwich

SERVES 2 ■ PREP TIME: 10 MINUTES, PLUS MARINATING TIME ■ COOK TIME: 17 MINUTES

This sandwich is a vegetarian version of the ever-popular Philly steak and cheese with all the same bold flavors, veggie topping, and melted provolone, just sans the steak. Portobello mushrooms are a delicious base, cooked to lightly caramelized perfection in the air fryer along with the bell pepper and onion. The air fryer is also used to melt the cheese and lightly crisp the buns for a meal fit for watching a Sunday football game.

3 tablespoons (45 ml) olive oil

3 tablespoons (45 ml) balsamic vinegar

1 teaspoon Worcestershire sauce

1 teaspoon dried parsley

½ teaspoon garlic powder

4 portobello mushrooms, stemmed and cut into ½-inch (1 cm) thick slices

1 green bell pepper, thinly sliced

1 small sweet onion, halved and thinly sliced

Sea salt

Freshly ground black pepper

Olive oil, for brushing

2 hoagie rolls, cut lengthwise without cutting right through

4 slices provolone cheese

1. In a medium bowl, whisk the oil, balsamic vinegar, Worcestershire sauce, parsley, and garlic powder until blended. Add the mushrooms, bell pepper, and onion and toss to coat. Season with salt and pepper, then set the vegetables aside at room temperature for at least 30 minutes.
2. Preheat on Air Fry at 360°F (185°C) for 3 minutes.
3. Brush the air fryer basket with oil and cook the vegetables in it for 12 to 15 minutes, until lightly caramelized on the edges, shaking the basket several times.
4. Pile the vegetables on the rolls and top with the cheese slices. Cook for 2 minutes or until the cheese is melted. Serve.

Sundried Tomato Pesto Kale Grilled Cheese

SERVES 2 ■ PREP TIME: 10 MINUTES ■ COOK TIME: 11 MINUTES

This is not a basic grilled cheese sandwich. Although it has only five ingredients, this recipe bursts with sundried tomato, sharp cheddar, and deep green kale. Grilled cheese sandwiches were the first thing I tried when I unpacked my air fryer, and every single time, the cheese was melted and the bread a glorious even brown. With that perfect, no-fail base, it is simple to experiment with other ingredients for tempting variations like this one.

1 cup (67 g) baby kale

2 tablespoons (28 g) butter, at room temperature

4 thick slices whole-grain bread

4 teaspoons (20 g) sundried tomato pesto

4 slices sharp cheddar

1. Place the kale in a microwave-safe dish with 1 teaspoon of water and microwave for 1 minute until wilted. Remove and squeeze out the excess moisture.
2. Preheat on Air Fry at 350°F (180°C) for 3 minutes.
3. Spread the butter evenly on one side of 2 slices of bread. Place them buttered-side down, in the air fryer basket and spread the tops of the slices with 1 teaspoon of pesto. Top with a slice of cheese, evenly spread half the wilted kale on each sandwich, and top with the remaining slices of cheese. Spread the remaining 2 teaspoons of pesto on one side of the remaining slices of bread and place them pesto-side down on the sandwich. Butter the tops of the last 2 slices and secure them with toothpicks.
4. Cook for 10 minutes, flipping the sandwiches over halfway through, until golden and the cheese is melted. Remove the toothpicks and serve.

This sandwich would be delicious with whole sundried tomatoes instead of pesto. Use the oil-packed product instead of dried to get the correct texture. Blot the extra oil off the tomatoes before using them in this sandwich.

Lunch

Don't let the lunch designation of these dishes limit when you eat them; these could also fit in beautifully for dinner or a snack. Some are more filling than others, like the flatbread pizza or pasties, but all are incredibly simple in your air fryer. Almost every recipe in this group can be adjusted to include other ingredients if you need to use something up or don't have a particular item on hand. So, have some fun and experiment with fillings and toppings for the dishes; you might create a new family favorite.

Loaded Flatbread Pizza

page 64

Melon Caprese Salad with Golden Goat Cheese

SERVES 4 ■ PREP TIME: 15 MINUTES ■ COOK TIME: 6 MINUTES

The air-fried goat cheese is the star of this dish, but the salad also deserves a standing ovation. Watermelon is one of my favorite foods, and although it is available year-round, the best, sweetest, deepest red melons are only found in the summer. I am a firm believer that seeded watermelons taste the best, but the seedless variety is probably better for this salad. Seeded watermelons hold a warm place in my heart because, as kids, we used to bestow the names of several coveted boys on the seeds, stick them to our foreheads, and the last seed to fall off was the boy we were going to marry. Don't scoff—my husband's watermelon seed hung on the longest when I was fourteen; obviously, watermelons are magic.

1 (8-ounce/225 g) log soft goat cheese, chilled

¼ cup (31 g) all-purpose flour

2 large eggs, beaten

¾ cup (90 g) breadcrumbs

Olive oil, for brushing

¼ seedless watermelon, cut into 1-inch (2 cm) cubes

½ cantaloupe, cut into 1-inch (2 cm) cubes

½ honeydew melon, cut into 1-inch (2 cm) cubes

¼ cup (60 ml) white balsamic vinegar

¼ cup (10 g) chiffonade fresh basil leaves

Sea salt

Freshly ground black pepper

1. Cut the goat cheese into 8 slices using fishing line or strong thread.
2. Place the flour in a small bowl, the eggs in a bowl next to the flour, and the breadcrumbs in a third bowl. Carefully dredge the goat cheese slices in the flour, then eggs, then breadcrumbs, coating the slices completely each time. Lightly brush them with oil on both sides.
3. Preheat on Air Fry at 390°F (195°C) for 3 minutes.
4. Cook the cheese for 6 minutes, turning halfway through, until golden brown.
5. While the cheese is cooking, in a large bowl, toss the melon cubes, balsamic vinegar, and basil. Season lightly with salt and pepper and arrange on 4 plates. Top the salads with 2 goat cheese slices each and serve.

You can use store-bought dressings for the salads in this book; just choose one closest to the flavors in the recipe.

Curried Roasted Cauliflower Salad

SERVES 4 ■ PREP TIME: 15 MINUTES ■ COOK TIME: 15 MINUTES

Cauliflower is the ideal vehicle for curry spices because it has a mild flavor and soaks up spices like a sponge. Tossed with a little oil, these florets become tender, crispy on the edges, and a pretty gold color when prepared in the air fryer. Potato chunks add interesting texture to this warm salad along with the tart, chewy cranberries. White cauliflower is the standard variety in most grocery stores, but you can also find orange and purple heads. They taste the same but can produce a splendid-looking dish for a potluck or family picnic.

1. In a large bowl, toss the cauliflower, potato, olive oil, curry powder, cumin, coriander, garlic powder, and cayenne pepper until well coated.
2. Preheat on Air Fry at 390°F (195°C) for 3 minutes.
3. Transfer the vegetables to the air fryer basket and cook 15 minutes, tossing halfway through, until tender.
4. While the cauliflower is cooking, whisk the coconut milk, tahini, lemon juice, maple syrup, and ginger until blended.
5. Transfer the cauliflower mixture to a large bowl and add the cranberries, scallion, and parsley. Toss in the dressing and serve.

Curried Roasted Cauliflower Salad

1 medium cauliflower head, cut into small florets

1 large russet potato, cut into ½-inch (1 cm) cubes

1 tablespoon (15 ml) olive oil

2 teaspoons curry powder

½ teaspoon ground cumin

¼ teaspoon ground coriander

½ teaspoon garlic powder

Pinch cayenne pepper

½ cup (60 g) dried cranberries

1 scallion, white and green parts, chopped

3 tablespoons (12 g) chopped fresh parsley

Dressing

3 tablespoons (45 g) coconut milk

3 tablespoons (45 g) tahini

Juice of ½ lemon

1 tablespoon (20 g) maple syrup

½ teaspoon peeled and grated ginger

Zucchini and Carrot Bhajis with Mixed Greens

SERVES 4 ■ PREP TIME: 15 MINUTES ■ COOK TIME: 30 MINUTES

Bhajis are crispy, spicy little bites made from shredded vegetables (usually, onion), served as an appetizer or side dish in Indian cuisine. I like to add them to a simple salad and use up the heaps of zucchini from my garden. You must squeeze out as much water as possible from the vegetables, and then squeeze out more, so they don't purge liquid while air frying. This would ruin the light, almost tempura-like texture of the bhajis.

3 medium zucchini, grated

2 small carrots, grated

¼ sweet onion, grated

1 cup (125 g) chickpea flour

1 large egg

1 teaspoon garam masala

¼ teaspoon ground cumin

¼ teaspoon sea salt

Oil spray

6 cups (180 g) mixed greens

½ cup (120 g) tahini dressing or buttermilk dressing

1. Place the zucchini, carrots, and onion in a clean kitchen cloth and squeeze out as much liquid as possible, twisting the top of the cloth. Place the vegetables in a large bowl and add the flour, egg, garam masala, cumin, and salt and stir until well mixed.
2. Preheat on Air Fry at 360°F (185°C) for 3 minutes.
3. Spray the basket with oil and, working in batches, scoop 2 tablespoon measures of the mixture into the basket in a single layer, about 6 per batch. Spray lightly with oil, and cook for 8 to 10 minutes, turning halfway through, until golden and crispy.
4. Repeat with the remaining mixture.
5. Arrange the greens on 4 plates and drizzle with the dressing. Serve with the warm bhajis.

Roasted Asparagus Farfalle Salad

SERVES 4 ■ PREP TIME: 10 MINUTES ■ COOK TIME: 10 MINUTES

Do you long for balmy evenings spent enjoying a leisurely al fresco meal on a patio or balcony? If so, this elegant salad can transport you with its earthy flavors and Mediterranean ingredients. Farfalle is my chosen pasta shape for salads because it is just fun; who doesn't love perky little bowties? And the scalloped edges and crevices of the shape capture all the flavors of the dressing, juices, roasted asparagus, and olives. Make sure you halve the tomatoes before air frying them; hot whole cherry tomatoes can burst violently when pierced by a fork.

½ cup (120 ml) store-bought balsamic dressing, divided

12 to 16 asparagus spears, woody ends trimmed, cut into 2-inch (5 cm) pieces

¼ red onion, cut into ½-inch (1 cm) chunks

20 cherry tomatoes, halved

4 cups (560 g) cooked farfalle pasta

¼ cup sliced, pitted Kalamata olives

¼ cup (25 g) shredded Parmesan cheese

2 tablespoons (5 g) chopped fresh basil

1. Preheat on Air Fry at 370°F (190°C) for 3 minutes.
2. In a large bowl, toss 2 tablespoons (30 ml) balsamic dressing, asparagus, and onion until well coated.
3. Transfer the vegetables to the air fryer basket and cook for 10 minutes, shaking once or twice, until tender. Add the cherry tomatoes halfway through the time.
4. Transfer the vegetables to a large bowl along with any juices in the bottom of the air fryer and add the remaining dressing, farfalle, olives, Parmesan cheese, and basil and toss to combine. Serve.

Loaded Flatbread Pizza

SERVES 2 ■ PREP TIME: 10 MINUTES ■ COOK TIME: 7 MINUTES

My husband was a professional hockey player for years, and pizza was a staple (it was the '80s; strict health wasn't a thing yet). He was a little blasé about the dish until I put this flatbread variation in front of him. The flatbread crust is more flavorful than regular pizza dough, and extremely convenient. The vegetarian toppings blend into a salty, sweet, hot, nutty, and peppery symphony in the mouth, and a thin layer of pesto adds complex taste but does not overpower the rest. My husband asks for this dish every week, and with my air fryer, I can make it in minutes.

1 (8-inch/20 cm) thin-crust flatbread

3 tablespoons (45 g) basil pesto, homemade or store-bought

1 medium tomato, thinly sliced

¼ cup (75 g) quartered marinated artichoke hearts

2 tablespoons (6 g) sliced black olives

Pinch red pepper flakes

½ cup (50 g) shaved Parmesan cheese

¼ cup (5 g) shredded arugula

1. Preheat on Air Fry at 370°F (190°C) for 3 minutes.
2. Spread the pesto on the flatbread all the way to the edges. Top the pizza with the tomato slices, artichoke hearts, and olives. Sprinkle with the red pepper flakes and the Parmesan cheese.
3. Place in the air fryer basket and cook until crispy and the cheese is melted, about 6 to 7 minutes.
4. Top with the arugula, cut into quarters, and serve.

Dutch Cheese Soufflé (Kaassoufflé)

SERVES 6 ■ PREP TIME: 20 MINUTES ■ COOK TIME: 20 MINUTES

My mother traveled from Canada to the Netherlands to see her family every couple of years when I was growing up, and when she came home, she always carried a huge wheel of gouda cheese in her suitcase. Looking back, this was wildly against customs regulations, but that cheese was sublime. This is my favorite recipe for gouda, and I rarely made it before my air fryer because I hate deep-frying. Now, these lovely little packets filled with melty, nutty gouda are ready in a snap, and my hair and house don't smell like oil all day.

2 (10x15-inch/25x38 cm) sheets puff pastry, thawed

6 (2x2x½-inch/5x5x1 cm) slices Gouda cheese

Water

2 large eggs, beaten

1 cup breadcrumbs

Avocado oil, for brushing

1. Using a sharp knife or pizza roller, cut each sheet of puff pastry into 6 squares.
2. Place half of the puff pastry squares on a clean work surface and put a slice of cheese in each square's center.
3. Brush the edges of the pastry squares with water and top each with another square, pressing lightly to seal tightly.
4. Place the beaten eggs in a small bowl next and the breadcrumbs in another.
5. Dredge the pastry squares in the egg and then the breadcrumbs, coating them completely.
6. Preheat on Air Fry at 340°F (175°C) for 3 minutes.
7. Lightly brush the breaded squares with oil and arrange half in the air fryer basket in a single layer. Cook until puffy and golden, about 10 minutes, turning halfway through. Repeat with the remaining squares and serve.

Black Bean Jalapeño Tostadas

SERVES 2 ■ PREP TIME: 10 MINUTES ■ COOK TIME: 26 MINUTES

In my first kitchen job as the dishwasher/salad prep girl at seventeen, I created crunchy edible salad bowls from scratch in the deep fryer with tortillas. I still have the scars to show for it. I did not know these fluted bowls were essentially tostadas (*toasted* in Spanish), and I could have avoided the multiple oil burns if air fryers had been available back then. You can use any type of tortilla, such as white flour, whole-wheat, corn, or multi-grain, for this flavor-packed meal. Corn is my favorite because it has a sweet taste, and the color of the finished tostada is terrific.

2 (6-inch/15 cm) flour or corn tortillas

Olive oil, for brushing

1 cup (170 g) canned low-sodium black beans, drained and rinsed

½ red bell pepper, diced

½ jalapeño pepper, seeded and chopped

½ teaspoon ground cumin

½ cup (75 g) crumbled queso fresco

1 tomato, diced

1 scallion, green part only, chopped

1 tablespoon (1 g) chopped fresh cilantro

1. Preheat on Air Fry at 370°F (190°C) for 3 minutes.
2. Brush the tortillas with oil on each side and cook one at a time in the air fryer basket for 8 minutes, until crispy, turning halfway through. Place a baking pan on top, so the tortilla does not blow around. Set the crispy tortillas aside.
3. In a 7-inch (18 cm) round baking pan, toss the beans, bell pepper, and jalapeño and cook for 12 to 15 minutes. Transfer the beans and vegetables with the cumin to a food processor and pulse until it is a coarse puree.
4. Spread the bean mixture onto each tostada and top with the cheese, tomato, scallion, and cilantro. Serve.

Savory Veggie Pasties

SERVES 12 ■ PREP TIME: 20 MINUTES ■ COOK TIME: 45 MINUTES

Pasties—handheld vegetable pies—are associated with Cornwall, and this vegetarian version uses puff pastry instead of short crust. You can certainly use a store-bought or homemade pie pastry for this tempting meal; the cooking time would be similar. These are lovely cold or hot and are the absolute perfect snack to tote along when watching a sports match or on a picnic or hike.

1 large sweet potato, peeled and cut into ½-inch (1 cm) cubes

1 large russet potato, peeled and cut into ½-inch (1 cm) cubes

1 tablespoon olive oil

Sea salt

Freshly ground black pepper

2 celery stalks, sliced

½ small onion, chopped

½ teaspoon minced garlic

1 cup (130 g) chopped frozen kale, thawed and squeezed out

½ cup (55 g) shredded Swiss cheese

1 teaspoon chopped fresh thyme

2 (10x15-inch/25x38 cm) sheets puff pastry, thawed

1 large egg, beaten

1. Place the sweet potato and potato in a 7-inch (18 cm) round baking pan and toss with the oil, salt, and pepper. Air Fry at 380°F (190°C) for 20 minutes, shaking once or twice, until very tender.
2. Add the celery, onion, and garlic, and cook for 5 minutes.
3. Transfer the vegetables to a medium bowl and stir in the kale, cheese, and thyme.
4. Place the puff pastry sheets on a clean work surface and cut each sheet into 6 (5-inch) squares with a sharp knife or pizza roller. Spoon the filling onto half of each square along the diagonal, leaving about ¼ inch around the edge.
5. In a small bowl, whisk the egg with 1 tablespoon of water and brush the edges of the pastry squares. Fold the other half of the squares over the filling to form triangles and press the edges firmly to seal.
6. Brush the pastries with the egg wash and cut three small slits in the top of each.
7. Preheat on Air Fry at 390°F (195°C) for 3 minutes.
8. Working in batches, cook the pastries in the air fryer basket until golden and puffy, 10 to 12 minutes. Serve hot, or cool completely before storing in a sealed container in the refrigerator for up to 3 days.

Instead of puff pastry, you can use pie crust (either store-bought or homemade) for these pies; it is actually more traditional. Cut the pie crust into the same size and use the same cooking time.

Red Pepper Black Olive Quesadillas

SERVES 2 ■ PREP TIME: 15 MINUTES ■ COOK TIME: 20 MINUTES

Quesadillas remind me of my long-ago Mexican honeymoon, and I picture white sand beaches, sparkling blue water, and margaritas the size of a mixing bowl whenever I eat these crispy creations. This version might seem too simple, but sometimes a few distinct, strong flavors like black olives, sweet roasted peppers, and robust spinach are enough to produce something exceptional. Feel free to switch the filling up with fresh tomatoes, salsa, jalapeños, beans, or goat cheese to suit your own palate, and you might imagine salt-kissed ocean breezes as well.

4 (6-inch/15 cm) flour tortillas

1 cup (115 g) shredded Mexican-blend cheese

½ cup (90 g) chopped jarred roasted red pepper

¼ cup (25 g) sliced black olives

1 cup (30 g) shredded baby spinach

2 tablespoons (8 g) chopped fresh oregano

Olive oil, for brushing

1. Preheat on Air Fry at 400°F (200°C) for 3 minutes.
2. Lay 2 tortillas on a clean work surface and evenly divide the cheese between them, sprinkling it to the edges. Top them evenly with the red pepper, olives, spinach, and oregano and cover with the remaining tortillas. Press down firmly.
3. Secure the quesadillas with 2 toothpicks each and brush both sides of each quesadilla with oil. Cook one at a time for 10 minutes, flipping halfway through, until golden brown and the cheese is melted.
4. Remove the toothpicks, cut the quesadillas into quarters, and serve.

Snacks and Appetizers

This chapter contains the type of food you probably think of when considering air frying. Lots of crunchy, breaded, pastry-wrapped finger foods ideal for nibbling while watching a game or served at a casual get-together on the patio. Some of my "memory" dishes are found here, those recipes that conjure a time or person when I take my first bite. Antojitos, qassatat, and wontons all flood me with lovely recollections, and I am grateful I can easily prepare them in my air fryer in minutes. I hope you create memories with a few of these snacks and appetizers and make them often for your loved ones.

Cheesy Pull-Apart Bread
page 94

Supplì al Telefono (Roman Rice Croquettes)

MAKES 12 RICE BALLS OR 4 TO 6 SERVINGS ■ PREP TIME: 30 MINUTES, PLUS CHILLING TIME ■ COOK TIME: 1 HOUR

This Roman bar snack's adorable name may soon be outdated. When you break open one of these fried rice croquettes, the mozzarella in the center stretches long and thin—just like an old-fashioned telephone cord. Hence *supplì al telefono*. No one has phones with cords anymore, but the cheese-pull on these supplì is nothing short of epic.

Supplì were intended as a use for leftover risotto. They are so tasty, however, that it is worth making a batch of risotto for no other purpose than to make it into these rice balls. You can also use leftover short-grain rice other than risotto, such as sushi rice.

1. Heat the stock in a small saucepan until simmering. Keep warm. In a Dutch oven, melt the butter over medium heat. Add the onion, season with salt, and sauté until softened, about 5 minutes. Add the rice and stir to coat with the butter. Cook the rice until slightly toasted, about 3 minutes. Add the wine and cook until the liquid has almost evaporated. Add 1 cup (240 ml) of the warm stock and stir to combine.
2. As the broth in the pan is absorbed by the rice, continue adding broth, a little bit at a time, stirring constantly. At first, the broth will be absorbed quickly, but as the rice becomes more saturated, it will absorb the broth more slowly and you will stir for longer before needing to add more. Keep the rice at a gentle simmer, adjusting the heat as necessary. Continue adding broth, stirring and waiting until the broth is absorbed before adding more, until the rice is tender, creamy, and cooked all the way through, about 20 minutes.
3. When the rice is done, add the grated Parmesan, lemon zest, 1 of the eggs, and salt and pepper to taste and stir to combine. Spread the risotto out on a sheet pan, cover, and chill in the refrigerator for at least 1 hour and as long as overnight.
4. While the risotto cools, make the tomato sauce. Heat the olive oil in a medium saucepan over medium heat. Add the garlic and red pepper flakes and cook for a minute. Add the crushed tomatoes and sugar and bring to a boil. Reduce the heat and simmer until thickened, about 15 minutes. Season with salt and pepper. Keep warm.

Rice Croquettes

3½ cups (840 ml) chicken or vegetable stock

4 tablespoons (55 g) unsalted butter

1 small yellow onion, minced

1 cup (195 g) Arborio rice

½ cup (120 ml) dry white wine

½ cup (50 g) grated Parmesan cheese

Zest of 1 lemon

3 eggs

2 ounces (55 g) fresh mozzarella cheese

¼ cup (32.5 g) peas, thawed if frozen

½ cup (63 g) all-purpose flour

1½ cups (75 g) panko breadcrumbs

Kosher salt

Freshly ground black pepper

Oil spray

Tomato Sauce

2 tablespoons (30 ml) extra-virgin olive oil

4 cloves garlic, minced

¼ teaspoon red pepper flakes

1 can (28 ounces/800 g) crushed tomatoes

2 teaspoons granulated sugar

Kosher salt

Freshly ground black pepper

5 Make the rice balls. Line a baking sheet with parchment paper. Form the risotto into twelve 2-inch (5 cm) balls. Flatten each ball into a disc and put a ½-inch (1 cm) piece of mozzarella and 5 to 6 peas in the center. Close the risotto around the filling and roll into a ball. Place the formed balls onto the baking sheet and chill until firm, at least 15 minutes.

6 Beat the remaining 2 eggs with 2 tablespoons (28 ml) of water. Place the flour on a small plate and spread the panko on a separate plate. Roll a rice ball in the flour, shaking off any excess, then coat with the egg mixture. Dredge the ball in the panko, pressing to make the crumbs adhere, and place the breaded rice ball on a lined baking sheet. Repeat with the remaining balls.

7 Spray the balls with oil and, working in batches, place 6 in a single layer in the air fryer basket. Air Fry at 400°F (200°C) for 10 to 12 minutes, flipping once halfway through, until browned and cooked through. Repeat with the remaining balls. Serve right away with warm tomato sauce.

Tofu Fries with Chili Lime Ketchup

SERVES 2 ■ PREP TIME: 15 MINUTES ■ COOK TIME: 20 MINUTES

Looking for a healthy alternative to your beloved potato fries and ketchup? Look no further than these lightly browned tofu batons for a filling snack or light meal. Air frying the tofu ensures the finish is perfect and the amount of oil minimal. Tossing the tofu in cornstarch creates a coating that crisps up, and the added spices infuse every bite. Don't skip the homemade ketchup dipping sauce; you might want to double the recipe because it is absolutely addictive.

Chili Lime Ketchup

½ cup (120 g) store-bought ketchup

1 tablespoon (15 g) brown sugar

1 tablespoon (15 ml) balsamic vinegar

Juice of ½ lime

¼ teaspoon red pepper flakes

Tofu Fries

1 tablespoon (8 g) cornstarch

1 teaspoon garlic powder

1 teaspoon dried oregano

½ teaspoon dried basil

½ teaspoon onion powder

¼ teaspoon ground paprika

¼ teaspoon sea salt

2 teaspoons olive oil

Oil spray

1(14-ounce/400 g) block extra-firm tofu, pressed (see page 30) and cut into ½-inch batons

1. In a small bowl, whisk together the ketchup, brown sugar, balsamic vinegar, lime juice, and red pepper flakes. Transfer the ketchup to an airtight container in the refrigerator for up to 2 weeks.
2. In a small bowl, toss the cornstarch, garlic powder, oregano, basil, onion powder, paprika, and salt until well mixed.
3. In a medium bowl, gently toss the tofu fries with the olive oil. Add the seasoning mix to the tofu and toss gently until well coated.
4. Preheat on Air Fry at 400°F (200°C) for 3 minutes. Lightly spray the air fryer basket with oil.
5. Working in batches, place the tofu fries in a single layer in the basket, lightly spray with oil, and cook for 10 minutes, shaking halfway through, until golden and crispy.
6. Repeat with the remaining fries and serve with the chili lime ketchup.

Maltese Ricotta Qassatat

SERVES 4 ■ PREP TIME: 20 MINUTES, PLUS CHILLING TIME ■ COOK TIME: 30 MINUTES

When you fly into Malta, there is a gut-dropping moment where no matter what window you look out of, it appears that the plane is descending into the sea. This small island located between Italy and North Africa was the only place to secure a visa for Libya in the '80s. While waiting for the bureaucratic red tape to untangle, often for days, we enjoyed the rich culture and food of this delightful country. Qassatat were my favorite snack at the sunny cafes at the seaside, so I had to try them in my air fryer thirty-five years later. The result wasn't entirely authentic, but certainly close enough that I briefly imagined the sparkling azure waters and scent of rich espresso at my first taste. Magnifico!

1½ cups (188 g) all-purpose flour

½ teaspoon baking powder

Pinch sea salt

½ cup (112 g) cold butter, cut into ½-inch (1 cm) cubes

Ice water

1 cup (250 g) whole-milk ricotta

2 small eggs, divided

⅛ teaspoon ground nutmeg

1. In a medium bowl, mix together the flour, baking powder, and salt until well blended. Add the butter and use your fingertips to rub it into the flour mixture, so it resembles coarse crumbs.
2. Sprinkle in cold water ½ teaspoon at a time until the dough holds together when pressed. Gather the dough into a ball, wrap it in plastic, and refrigerate for 30 minutes.
3. Roll the dough out until it is ⅛-inch (3 mm) thick, and cut it into 6- to 7-inch (15–18 cm) circles. Gather up any scraps and roll the dough out again to cut, until you have 8 circles.
4. In a small bowl, stir together the ricotta, 1 egg, and nutmeg.
5. Evenly divide the ricotta mixture among the dough circles, placing about 2 tablespoons (62–63 g) into each center.
6. Beat the remaining egg with 1 teaspoon of water and brush the mixture all around the pastry edges. Gather the edges over the filling, pleating it, and leaving the very center open.
7. Brush the outsides of the pastry with the beaten egg.
8. Preheat on Air Fry at 350°F (180°C) for 3 minutes.
9. Place 4 purses in the air fryer basket and cook for 15 minutes until the crust is golden. Repeat with the remaining purses.
10. Cool and serve.

Arepas Stuffed with Plantains and Feta Cheese

SERVES 3 ■ PREP TIME: 20 MINUTES, PLUS RESTING TIME ■ COOK TIME: 10 MINUTES

Arepa is an unleavened cornmeal-based bread shaped into small discs that are grilled, baked, or fried and can be eaten plain, stuffed, or split in half to form sandwiches, like this recipe. This bread is consumed daily in Columbia and Venezuela. If you can't find masarepa, look for enriched white cornmeal.

1½ cups (360 ml) warm water

2 teaspoons canola oil

¾ teaspoon sea salt

1½ cups (210 g) masarepa (pre-cooked yellow arepa flour)

Oil spray

¾ cup (112 g) crumbled feta cheese

1 large ripe plantain, thinly sliced

1 tomato, chopped

1 scallion, white and green parts, thinly sliced

1. In a medium bowl, combine the water, oil, and salt, stirring until the salt is dissolved. Add the flour in ½-cup (120 ml) measures, mixing to remove the lumps, until the dough holds together when pressed.
2. Cover the bowl and let the dough rest for 15 minutes.
3. Divide the dough into 6 equal pieces and form them into patties about ½-inch (1 cm) thick.
4. Preheat on Air Fry at 375°F (190°C) for 3 minutes. Lightly spray the patties with oil on both sides and place them in the air fryer basket. Cook, in batches if necessary, until golden brown and cooked through, about 10 minutes, turning halfway through.
5. Cool 10 minutes and then cut the arepas in half. Make sandwiches with the feta, plantains, tomato, and scallion, then serve.

Plantains can be found in most grocery stores, but they are usually green and unripe. Ripe plantains are yellow with a bit of black and firm to the touch. If you cannot find plantains, bananas can be substituted.

Roasted Vegetable Hummus

SERVES 4 ■ PREP TIME: 15 MINUTES ■ COOK TIME: 15 MINUTES

Hummus has become a mainstream product, but if you are over a certain age, you will remember when this humble dish was only seen in ethnic restaurants. What a shame it took so long for people to try this creamy, garlicky dip and even longer to start experimenting with other ingredients in their own kitchen. I have to admit that I disliked eggplant most of my life; it was this strange spongy vegetable with a bitter taste and often greasy texture due to its preparation. When you combine eggplant with the other vegetables in this recipe and air fry them to a perfect turn, the texture is silky, and the taste is mellow and rich. Try this dip tossed with pasta if you want a simple, appetizing meal in minutes.

½ small eggplant, halved lengthwise and cut into ½-inch (1 cm) cubes

1 zucchini, cut into ½-inch (1 cm) pieces

1 red bell pepper, cut into ½-inch (1 cm) pieces

½ red onion, cut into ½-inch (1 cm) pieces

2 garlic cloves, peeled and lightly crushed

1 tablespoon (15 ml) olive oil

1 (15-ounce/400 g) can low sodium chickpeas, drained and rinsed

Juice of ½ lemon

Sea salt

Freshly ground black pepper

Pita bread, cut vegetables, or tortilla chips, for serving

1. Preheat on Air Fry at 375°F (190°C) for 3 minutes.
2. In a large bowl, toss the eggplant, zucchini, bell pepper, onion, garlic, and oil until the vegetables are coated.
3. Season lightly with salt and pepper and transfer them to the air fryer basket. Cook for 12 to 15 minutes, tossing once or twice, until tender and lightly caramelized.
4. Transfer the vegetables and any juices accumulated in the bottom of the air fryer into a food processor. Add the chickpeas and lemon juice and process until smooth.
5. Season with salt and pepper and serve with your preferred dippers.
6. Store the dip in a sealed container in the refrigerator for up to 4 days.

Spicy Roasted Chickpeas

SERVES 4 ■ PREP TIME: 10 MINUTES ■ COOK TIME: 12 MINUTES

Chickpeas don't look like they can be a satisfying snack; when you open the can or boil them, these legumes are soft and plump. Air frying chickpeas is quick, and they turn out incredibly crispy and golden with very little oil. They are a better choice than chips or other junk food and will satisfy your craving for salt and crunch. The combination of spices in this recipe can be changed up to anything you want, or you can fry plain chickpeas accented with a little sea salt.

1 (15-ounce/400 g) can chickpeas, drained, rinsed, and patted dry

1 tablespoon (15 ml) olive oil, plus extra for brushing

½ teaspoon sea salt

¼ teaspoon harissa powder

¼ teaspoon garlic powder

1. In a medium bowl, mix together the chickpeas, oil, salt, harissa, and garlic powder.
2. Preheat on Roast at 390°F (195°C) for 3 minutes.
3. Lightly brush the air fryer basket with oil and spread the chickpeas in a single layer. Roast for 12 minutes, tossing halfway through.
4. Cool and serve.
5. Store in an airtight container at room temperature for up to 3 days.

Sweet Potato Tots with Sriracha Mayonnaise

SERVES 4 ■ PREP TIME: 15 MINUTES ■ COOK TIME: 40 MINUTES

Tater tots never passed my house's threshold when growing up because my European mother could not fathom this product. As a chef, I also turned up my nose at frozen convenience food until I prepared a very highfalutin dish called duchess potatoes, which is piped mashed potatoes cooked to a crispy golden brown. We once ended up with thicker mashed potatoes than usual, and my executive chef piped short rows instead of rosettes. When baked—voilà—tater tots. This recipe subs in sweet potato and takes a shortcut in an air fryer, but my chef would have been proud to serve them, especially with the fiery mayo dipping sauce.

Sriracha Mayonnaise

½ cup (115 g) mayonnaise

2 tablespoons (30 g) sriracha

Juice of ½ lime

Sweet Potato Tots

2 large sweet potatoes, peeled and quartered

½ teaspoon chopped fresh thyme

½ teaspoon sea salt

Oil spray

1. In a small bowl, mix together the mayonnaise, sriracha, and lime juice until well blended. Set aside.
2. Place the sweet potatoes in a large saucepan and cover them by 2 inches (5 cm) of cold water. Bring to a boil over high heat, reduce the heat to medium-low, and simmer until they are about halfway cooked, about 10 minutes.
3. Drain and let the potatoes cool until they can be handled, about 10 minutes. Grate the sweet potatoes on the large side of a box grater into a medium bowl. Add the thyme and salt and toss to combine.
4. Scoop out tablespoon measures of the sweet potatoes and form them into tots, either round or oblong. Set the tots aside for about 10 minutes.
5. Preheat on Air Fry at 375°F (190°C) for 3 minutes. Lightly spray the air fryer basket with oil and, working in batches if necessary, place the tots in a single layer in the basket and lightly spray them with oil.
6. Cook for 15 minutes, shaking every 5 minutes, until golden. Transfer the cooked tots to a plate and repeat with the remaining tots. Serve with sriracha mayonnaise.

Soft Pretzel Bites with Cheesy Beer Dipping Sauce

SERVES 4 ■ PREP TIME: 30 MINUTES, PLUS RISING TIME ■ COOK TIME: 20 MINUTES, PLUS BOILING TIME

You probably think this recipe looks fiddly—who wants to mess with yeast and rising times? I can assure you, every second spent making these deep-brown, salt-decorated pretzels is worth it, especially when you taste them with the beer-spiked sauce. The trick to the signature taste and wonderful colored pretzel crust is a baking soda bath before baking. Not for you, for the dough! If you don't feel like twisting the dough into classic pretzel shapes, you can make knots or braid the pieces. Just make sure all the ends are firmly pressed together, so your chosen shape doesn't fly apart in the simmering water.

Soft Pretzel Bites

1 cup (235 ml) warm water, 105 to 115°F (41 to 46°C)

2 teaspoons sugar

1 teaspoon sea salt

2 teaspoons active dry yeast

3 cups (375 g) all-purpose flour

3 tablespoons (45 g) melted butter

Oil spray

4 quarts (3¾ liters) water

½ cup (110 g) baking soda

1 large egg, beaten with 1 teaspoon water

1 tablespoon (18 g) coarse sea salt

Cheesy Beer Dip

2 tablespoons (28 g) unsalted butter

2 tablespoons (16 g) all-purpose flour

¾ cup (175 ml) whole milk

½ cup (120 ml) dark beer

1½ cups (170 g) shredded sharp cheddar

Sea salt

1. In a large bowl, mix together the water, sugar, and salt and sprinkle the yeast on top. Let stand for 10 minutes until foamy.
2. Add the flour and butter and mix until combined. Turn the dough out on a lightly floured work surface and knead until it is smooth and elastic, about 10 minutes. You can also use a stand mixer with a dough hook.
3. Lightly oil a large bowl and gather the dough into a ball. Place the dough in the bowl, cover with a clean cloth, and set in a warm place to rise until it has doubled in size, about 1 hour.
4. While the dough is rising, melt the butter in a medium saucepan over medium-high heat. Add the flour and whisk until a paste forms and the flour cooks out, about 1 minute.
5. Reduce the heat to medium, add the milk and beer, and whisk until the sauce is thick and smooth, about 2 minutes. Whisk in the cheese until it is melted and the dip is smooth. Season with salt and set aside.
6. While the dough is rising, bring the water to a boil in a large pot over medium-high heat. With the water boiling, add the baking soda in small quantities until the full amount is used. Do not just dump it in because the mixture will foam up. Spray a baking sheet with oil and set aside.
7. When the rise is complete, divide the dough into 4 equal pieces. Roll each piece of dough into a 1-inch (2.5 cm) thick rope and cut the dough into 1½-inch (3.5 cm) pieces. Working in batches if necessary, place the pretzel bites in the water and simmer for 30 seconds.
8. With a slotted spoon, remove the bites from the water and transfer them to the baking sheet. Pat the excess water off the dough, brush with egg, and sprinkle with the coarse salt.
9. Preheat on Air Fry at 390°F (195°C) for 3 minutes. Lightly spray the basket with oil and, working in batches, place the pretzel bites in a single layer in the basket, about 2 inches (5 cm) apart.
10. Cook for 8 to 10 minutes, until they are an even brown. Repeat with the remaining bites. Serve with warm cheesy beer dipping sauce.

Antojitos

SERVES 4 ■ PREP TIME: 15 MINUTES ■ COOK TIME: 12 MINUTES

For almost twenty-five years, there was a small, bistro-style restaurant called the Babel Fish in downtown Guelph, Ontario, Canada. I first tried antojitos sitting at their charming mismatched tables looking at eclectic local art. The creamy, cheesy, crispy pinwheels with the slow-building heat from jalapeños and cayenne were exceptional and addictive. This flavorful dish is one of the first recipes I tried in my air fryer, and it brought back lovely memories.

1 (8-ounce/225 g) block cream cheese, at room temperature

½ cup (60 g) finely diced red bell pepper

¼ cup (30 g) finely diced jalapeño pepper

1 scallion, white and green parts, finely diced

1 tablespoon (1 g) finely chopped fresh cilantro

⅛ teaspoon cayenne pepper

Salt sea

Freshly ground black pepper

2 (8-inch/20 cm) flour tortillas

1 cup (120 g) shredded cheddar cheese

Sour cream, for serving

1. In a medium bowl, combine the cream cheese, bell pepper, jalapeño, scallion, cilantro, and cayenne until well mixed and season with salt and pepper.
2. Place the tortillas on a clean work surface and evenly divide the filling between them. Spread the filling right to the tortilla edges and sprinkle the shredded cheese on top, dividing it between them.
3. Roll up a tortilla firmly starting at the end closest to you, placing it seam-side down as you roll the remaining tortilla. Cut a tortilla on a bias into 1½-inch (3.5 cm) -wide slices and place them in a 7-inch (18 cm) round baking pan. The end pieces will be uneven, but you can use them anyway. Cut the remaining tortilla and cover with plastic wrap so the pieces don't dry out.
4. Preheat on Air Fry at 350°F (180°C) for 3 minutes.
5. Cook the tortillas for 5 to 6 minutes, or until crisp and golden. Remove and repeat with the remaining tortillas.
6. Serve with sour cream.

If you want to ensure your pinwheels do not unroll during cooking, secure them with toothpicks. Just make sure you remove them before eating!

Sicilian Caponata

SERVES 4 ■ PREP TIME: 20 MINUTES, PLUS RESTING TIME ■ COOK TIME: 12 MINUTES

This is basically a sweet-and-sour stew, packed with vegetables, olives, and capers, served as an appetizer or side dish. This variation adds pine nuts for crunch, balsamic vinegar and brown sugar for sweetness, and cocoa powder for depth and richness of flavor. The traditional caponata elements are cooked separately and then combined, and the air fryer produces perfectly tender eggplant for this recipe. Try tossing warm caponata with cooked pasta or zucchini noodles as a filling main course.

1 pound (455 g) eggplant, cut into 1-inch (2 cm) pieces

1 teaspoon sea salt

½ red onion, cut into ¼-inch (5 mm) slices

1 tablespoon (15 ml) olive oil

1 cup (240 g) canned crushed tomatoes (San Marzano if possible)

2 tablespoons (30 ml) balsamic vinegar

1 tablespoon (15 g) brown sugar

1 teaspoon cocoa powder

¼ cup (25 g) chopped green olives

2 tablespoons (5 g) chopped basil

1 tablespoon (9 g) vinegar-marinated capers

1 tablespoon (9 g) pine nuts

Sea salt

Freshly ground black pepper

1. Place the eggplant in a strainer and toss with the salt. Let the eggplant sit in the sink or over a bowl for 1 to 2 hours. Rinse the eggplant with cold water and pat dry with paper towels.
2. Preheat on Air Fry at 375°F (190°C) for 3 minutes.
3. Place the eggplant and onion in the air fryer basket and drizzle with oil. Toss to coat.
4. Cook for 10 to 12 minutes, tossing once or twice, until tender and lightly caramelized.
5. While the eggplant is cooking, place the crushed tomato, balsamic vinegar, brown sugar, and cocoa powder in a medium saucepan over medium heat and bring to a simmer. Partially cover, reduce the heat to low, and simmer for 5 minutes. Transfer the sauce to a large bowl.
6. When the vegetables are cooked, transfer them to the bowl with the tomato sauce and stir in the olives, basil, capers, and pine nuts.
7. Cover and refrigerate the caponata overnight to mellow the flavors. Taste, season with salt and pepper, and serve with your favorite dippers.

Mixed Vegetable Wontons

SERVES 4 ■ PREP TIME: 15 MINUTES ■ COOK TIME: 25 MINUTES

As a child, I looked forward to ordering wontons at the local Chinese restaurant; they were the only dish I wanted every visit. Crispy, golden, delightfully bubbly wrappers cradled finely shredded vegetables flavored with lush sesame oil. Since we couldn't make these delights at home, I only enjoyed wontons every six months or so. With my air fryer, wontons can be a daily treat if I desire, and can be whipped up in less than thirty minutes. This version uses sesame oil like the ones from my youth and tastes fabulous.

2 teaspoons sesame oil

1 teaspoon minced garlic

1 teaspoon peeled and grated fresh ginger

1 cup (70 g) finely shredded napa cabbage

1 carrot, finely shredded

½ cup (25 g) bean sprouts, coarsely chopped

1 scallion, white and green parts, finely chopped

1 tablespoon (8 g) sesame seeds

½ teaspoon soy sauce

Pinch red pepper flakes

1 large egg

1 tablespoon (15 ml) water

16 wonton wrappers

Oil spray

1. Heat the oil in a large skillet over medium-high heat. Sauté the garlic and ginger until fragrant, about 2 minutes.
2. Add the cabbage, carrot, bean sprouts, and scallion and sauté until tender-crisp, about 4 minutes. Remove from the heat and stir in the sesame seeds, soy sauce, and red pepper flakes.
3. Beat the egg and water in a small bowl until well blended.
4. Place a wonton wrapper on your work surface and use your fingertips to brush the edges with the egg mixture. Place about 1½ teaspoons of the filling in the center of the wrapper and fold one of the corners over the filling to form a triangle. Press the air out and seal the triangle tightly. Repeat with the remaining wonton wrappers.
5. Preheat on Air Fry at 350°F (180°C) for 3 minutes. Lightly oil the air fryer basket.
6. Working in batches, place the wontons in a single layer in the basket and spray them with oil. Cook for 4 minutes, flip them over and spray with oil, and cook for 5 minutes longer or until crispy and golden.
7. Repeat with the remaining wontons and serve.

Elote Dip with Tortilla Chips

SERVES 4 ■ PREP TIME: 10 MINUTES ■ COOK TIME: 30 MINUTES

If you follow food trends at all, you will know that street food is a passion for many, and elote (street corn cobs) is at the top of the most-wanted world food list. This dip takes all those lovely flavors—grilled corn, hot peppers, lime, and cotija cheese—and combines them into a tempting appetizer. The golden tortilla chips and the dip are prepared in the air fryer with little effort and time. You can put the dip together ahead and store it in the refrigerator until serving. If you cook it directly from the fridge, add five to ten minutes to the cooking time to ensure it is bubbly and the cheese is melted.

8 (6-inch/15 cm) corn tortillas

1 tablespoon (15 ml) canola oil, divided

2 cups (260 g) frozen corn kernels, thawed

1 jalapeño pepper, finely chopped

⅓ cup (77 g) sour cream

2 tablespoons (28 g) mayonnaise

Juice of 1 lime

½ teaspoon chipotle chili powder

1 cup (150 g) crumbled cotija cheese

1. Brush the tortillas lightly with oil and cut each into 6 wedges.
2. Preheat on Air Fry at 400°F (200°C) for 3 minutes.
3. Working in batches, spread the chips in a single layer in the basket and cook until crispy, about 5 minutes, turning halfway through. Remove to a plate to cool and repeat with the remaining tortilla chips. Set aside.
4. Toss the corn and jalapeño with the remaining oil in a 7-inch (18 cm) round baking pan and cook for 10 minutes, until lightly browned, stirring halfway through.
5. Lower the temperature to 370°F (190°C). Stir in the sour cream, mayonnaise, lime juice, chili powder, and three-quarters of the cotija cheese. Top with the remaining cheese and cook for 10 minutes or until the cheese is melted and the dip is lightly browned and bubbly.
6. Serve with the tortilla chips.

Try fresh corn cut right off the cob instead of frozen. You can air fry the cobs to create a lovely taste. Lightly oil the husked corn and place the cobs in the basket. Air fry at 400°F (200°C) for 10 minutes, turning halfway through. Wait 10 minutes for the corn to cool and then cut the kernels off the cob.

Avocado Chipotle Deviled Eggs

MAKES 12 ■ PREP TIME: 15 MINUTES ■ COOK TIME: 11 MINUTES

I have a confession: I love deviled eggs. These little beauties were staples at almost every potluck dinner, picnic, and cocktail party while growing up in the '70s. My job was to whip the yolks with whatever ingredients my mom wanted, usually just mayo, salt, and pepper but sometimes very daring curry. This pale green, spicy version would have been shocking to that retro crowd but is very on-trend in today's culinary climate. The fact you can make perfect hardboiled eggs in an air fryer was the biggest revelation for me, and that benefit alone is worth buying this handy kitchen tool.

6 large eggs

½ avocado

¼ cup (60 g) mayonnaise

Juice of ½ lemon

2 tablespoons (2 g) minced cilantro

¼ teaspoon chipotle chili powder

Sea salt

Freshly ground black pepper

1. Place the wire rack that comes with most air fryers in the basket and place the eggs onto the rack. If you have no rack, place the eggs directly in the basket. Air fry at 300°F (150°C) for 11 minutes.
2. Remove the eggs to a medium bowl filled with ice and water to stop the cooking process.
3. When the eggs are cool, peel them, and cut them lengthwise in half.
4. Scoop out the yolks, place them in a medium bowl, and set the whites on a serving plate.
5. Add the avocado to the bowl and mash with the yolks until well blended and smooth. Stir in the mayonnaise, lemon juice, cilantro, and chili powder. Season lightly with salt and pepper.
6. Spoon the yolk mixture back into the hollows in the whites. Serve immediately or store in a sealed container in the refrigerator for up to 1 day.

You can also create some interesting variations for deviled eggs, depending on the ingredients added to the yolk filling. You can keep it traditional with mayonnaise and paprika, or try chili powder, dill, curry, sundried tomatoes, or pesto.

Cheesy Pull-Apart Bread

SERVES 6 ■ PREP TIME: 10 MINUTES ■ COOK TIME: 7 MINUTES

I cannot describe how decadent this easy-to-prepare bread tastes and how pretty it looks as a centerpiece for guests and family. The trick is to cut the center of the bread into perfect squares, shallow enough so the bread stays together and deep enough to stuff lots of scrumptious cheese into the crevices. Look for real buffalo milk mozzarella created using a process called *pasta filata* where the milk is spun into strands and cut. This product has the perfect texture and an unbeatable fresh taste.

⅓ cup (75 g) melted butter

1 scallion, white and green parts, finely chopped

½ teaspoon garlic powder

1 teaspoon dried oregano

Sea salt

Freshly ground black pepper

1 cup (120 g) shredded mozzarella

½ cup (60 g) shredded cheddar cheese

½ cup (60 g) shredded Gouda cheese

1 loaf crusty bread that fits easily in your air fryer

1. In a small bowl, stir together the melted butter, scallion, garlic powder, and oregano. Season lightly with salt and pepper and set aside.
2. In another small bowl, toss together the mozzarella, cheddar, and gouda and set aside.
3. With a serrated knife, cut the bread in a crosshatch diagonal pattern of 1-inch diamonds, about 2- to 3-inches deep depending on the bread's size, leaving about ½ inch of uncut bread on the sides.
4. Preheat on Air Fry at 350°F (180°C) for 3 minutes.
5. Pour the melted butter mixture over the top of the bread, making sure it seeps into all the crevices. Top the bread with the cheese, pushing the shreds into the crevices as much as possible.
6. Place the bread in the air fryer basket and cook for 5 to 7 minutes until golden and warmed through, and the cheese is melted.
7. Serve.

Sides

Side dishes in plant-based cuisine are often smaller versions of the main courses, which can be confusing. Can you eat some of these recipes as a full meal? Certainly, but they are designed to accompany other dishes, so they are not overly complicated. The Johnny cakes and fry bread are ideal dippers for stew, soups, and casseroles. The spaghetti squash and baked fennel can be topped with ratatouille, chili, or lentil "meatballs." And the veggie packets and cauliflower bake would be delicious next to stir-fries and eggplant paprikash, respectively. Mix and match textures and flavors to create exciting possibilities, and you will never get bored at mealtime.

Cheesy Cauliflower Bake page 106

Fried Green Tomatoes with Rémoulade

SERVES 4 ■ PREP TIME: 15 MINUTES, PLUS CHILLING TIME
■ COOK TIME: 30 MINUTES

Gardeners and farmers market devotees are often confronted with piles of green tomatoes at the end of summer. Recently, I have noticed them in grocery stores year-round. What better way to use up these firm, tart unripe tomatoes than to batter them and fry them?

The air fryer makes it easy to enjoy fried green tomatoes any time of year without heating up a pot of oil or, as is traditional, bacon grease. These are best enjoyed hot, right out of the air fryer, with a tangy dipping sauce, such as this Louisiana-style rémoulade. Fried green tomatoes work on their own as a side dish for grilled steak or chicken, but you can also add them to a salad or even put them in a sandwich. Try a fried green tomato slider or a fried green tomato BLT.

1. Combine all the rémoulade ingredients in a medium-size bowl. Cover and chill for at least 1 hour to allow the flavors to develop.
2. To make the fried green tomatoes, trim the ends off each tomato and slice into ¼-inch-thick (5 mm) slices. Place the slices on a paper towel–lined plate to absorb excess liquid.
3. Place the flour, cornmeal, salt, black pepper, and cayenne pepper on a second plate, stirring with a fork to combine. Whisk the eggs and buttermilk together in a shallow bowl.
4. Dip a third of the tomato slices in the egg mixture then dredge them in the flour-cornmeal mixture, shaking off any excess. (Do not coat the tomato slices until right before you cook them.) Spray both sides with oil, making sure to coat the slices well. Place the slices in the basket of the air fryer and Air Fry at 400°F (200°C) for 10 minutes, flipping the slices once halfway through. (If you see spots that look like dry flour, spray those with additional oil.) While the first batch of tomatoes is cooking, batter the next batch. Repeat the process with the remaining slices.
5. Serve the fried green tomatoes hot out of the fryer with rémoulade sauce.

Rémoulade

1 cup (225 g) mayonnaise

3 tablespoons (45 g) mustard

1 tablespoon (15 ml) freshly squeezed lemon juice

1 tablespoon (8.6 g) capers

1 tablespoon (1.3 g) chopped fresh flat-leaf parsley

2 scallions, white and light green part only, sliced

2 teaspoons Louisiana-style hot sauce

1½ teaspoons Cajun seasoning

½ teaspoon garlic powder

½ teaspoon freshly ground black pepper

Fried Green Tomatoes

3 green tomatoes

¾ cup (94 g) all-purpose flour

¾ cup (105 g) cornmeal, preferably finely ground

1½ teaspoons kosher salt

1 teaspoon freshly ground black pepper

½ teaspoon cayenne pepper

2 eggs

¼ cup (60 ml) buttermilk (regular milk is an acceptable substitute)

Oil spray

Golden Johnny Cakes

SERVES 4 ■ PREP TIME: 10 MINUTES ■ COOK TIME: 25 MINUTES

Johnny cakes were traditionally cornmeal gruel—thick porridge—fried in a cast-iron skillet, ideal for filling bellies on long trips. This version still features cornmeal but is more tender and biscuit-like than the original. I recommend baking the batter in a baking pan for convenience, but it can also be rolled into balls, flattened into disks, and cooked on a flat, round air fryer baking sheet. Lightly oil the cakes to get a lovely golden finish.

Canola oil, for greasing

1 cup (125 g) all-purpose flour

1 cup (140 g) yellow cornmeal

3 tablespoons (39 g) granulated sugar

1 tablespoon (14 g) baking powder

¼ teaspoon salt

1 cup (235 ml) milk

2 large eggs, beaten

1. Lightly grease a 7-inch (18 cm) round baking pan with oil.
2. In a medium bowl, mix the flour, cornmeal, sugar, baking powder, and salt until well blended. Make a well in the center and add the milk and eggs, stirring until just combined.
3. Transfer the batter to the baking pan and tap it on the counter to remove any air bubbles.
4. Preheat on Air Fry at 375°F (190°C) for 3 minutes.
5. Cook the johnny cake until a knife inserted in the center comes out clean and it is golden brown, about 20 to 25 minutes.
6. Cut into 4 or 8 pieces and serve warm, slathered with butter, with chili or soup.

Scalloped Corn with Jalapeños

SERVES 4 ■ PREP TIME: 10 MINUTES ■ COOK TIME: 25 MINUTES

The corn in this rich-tasting recipe is not actually scalloped (meaning "thinly sliced" in old English), but the creamy, onion-infused sauce fits the bill of dishes similar to this one that do use scalloped vegetables. Corn and jalapeños are a classic pairing in Southwestern-style foods, and they work beautifully here. This flavorful casserole is perfect with vegetable kebabs eaten outdoors on a warm summer evening. You can whip up this dish in your air fryer while barbecuing your skewers, and your kitchen will stay cool and clean.

Canola oil, for greasing

2 (12-ounce/340 g) cans whole kernel corn, drained

¼ jalapeño pepper, chopped

¼ small sweet onion, chopped

¾ cup (175 ml) whole milk

½ cup (60 g) panko breadcrumbs

1 large egg, beaten

2 tablespoons (28 g) melted butter, plus extra for greasing

Sea salt

Freshly ground black pepper

1. Lightly grease a 7-inch (18 cm) round baking pan with oil.
2. Preheat the air fryer on Roast at 330°F (170°C) for 3 minutes.
3. In a large bowl, combine the corn, jalapeño pepper, onion, milk, breadcrumbs, egg, and butter until well combined. Season with salt and pepper.
4. Transfer the mixture to the baking pan. Cook for 25 minutes or until the center is set.
5. Serve warm.

Asian Vegetable Packet

SERVES 2 ■ PREP TIME: 20 MINUTES ■ COOK TIME: 15 MINUTES

Cooking different ingredients in packets, either with foil or the traditional parchment paper, is a French method called *en papillote*. The benefit of this preparation is all the flavors and juices stay in the packet, so the finished dish is packed with delightful taste and moistness. Air frying ensures even heat and quick cooking time, so these soy, ginger, and honey–accented veggies turn out perfect every time. Just take care when opening the packet because the escaping steam can burn.

4 small bok choy heads, quartered

1 red bell pepper, cut into 1-inch (2 cm) pieces

1 scallion, white and green parts, sliced

1 cup (70 g) broccoli florets

1 cup (200 g) canned baby corn, cut into 2-inch (5 cm) pieces

1 cup (100 g) snow peas, stringed and halved

2 tablespoons (30 ml) low-sodium soy sauce

2 tablespoons (40 g) honey

1 teaspoon peeled and grated fresh ginger

½ teaspoon minced garlic

Pinch of red pepper flakes

1 teaspoon sesame seeds, for garnish

1. Drape 2 pieces of aluminum foil in a 7-inch (18 cm) round baking pan, one on top of each other in a cross. The entire pan should be covered
2. Place the bok choy, bell pepper, scallion, broccoli, corn, and snow peas in the baking pan, tossing to combine.
3. In a small bowl, stir together the soy sauce, honey, ginger, garlic, and red pepper flakes. Drizzle it evenly over the vegetables. Fold the foil up around the vegetables to form a tightly sealed packet.
4. Preheat the air fryer on Roast at 350°F (180°C) for 3 minutes.
5. Cook for 15 minutes until the vegetables are tender.
6. Open the packet carefully to avoid the escaping steam, garnish with sesame seeds, and serve.

Caramelized Maple Celeriac

SERVES 4 ■ PREP TIME: 10 MINUTES ■ COOK TIME: 20 MINUTES

I love celeriac, or celery root; it has a mild flavor that combines well with both sweet and savory ingredients, and it caramelizes beautifully in very little time in an air fryer. This recipe is on the sweeter side because of the natural sugars in the vegetable and, of course, the added maple syrup. You can also create a savory side dish by excluding the syrup and tossing with garlic powder, fennel seed, or paprika. Celery root is even delicious with just olive oil and a light seasoning of salt and pepper, so try several versions to get the best for you.

2 small celeriac roots, peeled and cut into 1-inch (2 cm) pieces

1 teaspoon olive oil

2 tablespoons (40 g) maple syrup

¼ teaspoon ground cinnamon

¼ teaspoon ground nutmeg

Sea salt

Freshly ground black pepper

1. In a large bowl, toss together the celeriac, olive oil, maple syrup, cinnamon, and nutmeg.
2. Preheat the air fryer on Roast at 375° (190°C) for 3 minutes.
3. Transfer the celeriac to a 7-inch (18 cm) round baking pan (3-inches/7.5 cm) deep). Roast for about 20 minutes, or until very tender and lightly caramelized, tossing halfway through.
4. Season with salt and pepper and serve.

Maple syrup comes in different grades that reflect the flavor and appearance. Check the label of the syrup to make sure the product is pure rather than cut with corn syrup. Look for Grade A Dark Amber or Canadian #3 Dark (D) for the best product.

Cheesy Cauliflower Bake

SERVES 4 ■ PREP TIME: 10 MINUTES ■ COOK TIME: 17 MINUTES

Cauliflower with cheese sauce is a regular addition to my holiday table spread, and I often end up muttering swear words and regretting the choice because it is a pain to prepare. It's usually the last thing to do because the cauliflower needs to be tender but not mushy, and the sauce requires supervision and another pot, so more dishes. So inconvenient! Imagine my relief when I discovered that you can make a very similar cheesy recipe in less than thirty minutes in the air fryer with no supervision or pile of dishes. Try your favorite nondairy cheese for a tasty vegan option.

1 small head cauliflower, cut into small florets

2 teaspoons olive oil

¼ teaspoon onion powder

¼ teaspoon garlic powder

½ cup (60 g) shredded cheddar cheese

Freshly ground black pepper

1 tablespoon (4 g) chopped fresh parsley

1. Preheat on Air Fry at 375°F (190°C) for 3 minutes.
2. In a medium bowl, toss the cauliflower, oil, onion powder, and garlic powder until well coated.
3. Transfer the cauliflower to the air fryer basket and cook for 12 minutes until lightly caramelized and tender, tossing halfway through.
4. Transfer the cauliflower to a 7-inch (18 cm) round baking pan and top with the cheddar. Cook for 5 minutes until the cheese is melted.
5. Season with pepper and serve topped with parsley.

Herbed Spaghetti Squash with Garlic and Parmesan

SERVES 4 ■ PREP TIME: 10 MINUTES ■ COOK TIME: 20 MINUTES

Spaghetti squash was not something my mother ever cooked; I didn't encounter this vegetable until I switched to an ill-conceived weight loss diet and wanted a pasta substitute. The diet soon fell by the wayside because I wanted energy to actually move around, but this charming, noodle-textured vegetable remained a favorite of mine. I made it in the oven in the past, and it took a long time to cook down, but in the air fryer, I can enjoy this dish in less than thirty minutes. Try adding a spoonful or two of pesto, a scoop of hot tomato sauce, or sautéed mushrooms if you want to switch up the basic recipe.

1 (2-pound/1 kg) spaghetti squash

1 teaspoon olive oil

½ cup (40 g) shredded Parmesan cheese

2 tablespoons (28 g) butter

¼ teaspoon garlic powder

2 tablespoons (5 g) chopped fresh basil

Sea salt

Freshly ground black pepper

1. Preheat on Air Fry at 370°F (190°C) for 3 minutes.
2. Cut the squash in half lengthwise and scoop out the seeds.
3. Place the halves cut-side up in the air fryer basket and drizzle with the oil. Cook for 15 to 18 minutes until the squash is tender.
4. Remove the squash from the air fryer and use a fork to shred the flesh into a medium bowl.
5. Add the Parmesan, butter, garlic, and basil and toss until the squash is coated. Season with salt and pepper and serve.

Baked Fennel with Pesto Breadcrumb Topping

SERVES 4 ■ PREP TIME: 10 MINUTES ■ COOK TIME: 20 MINUTES

I use fennel a great deal because I love the anise flavor, which deepens when roasted or cooked in an air fryer. The pesto topping bolsters that wonderful characteristic because basil has a hint of licorice as well. This recipe can be a fabulous side dish for vegan or vegetarian meatballs or a nice lentil "meatloaf." If you need a gluten-free version, substitute ground almonds for the breadcrumbs.

1 large fennel bulb, halved and cut into 1-inch (2 cm) slices

½ sweet onion, thinly sliced

1 tablespoon olive oil

Sea salt

Freshly ground black pepper

½ cup (60 g) panko breadcrumbs

¼ cup (25 g) grated Parmesan cheese

2 tablespoons (30 g) basil pesto

1. In a medium bowl, toss the fennel, onion, and olive oil until well coated. Season lightly with salt and pepper and transfer the vegetables to the air fryer basket.
2. Air Fry at 370°F (190°C) for 15 minutes until lightly caramelized and tender, tossing halfway through.
3. In a small bowl, stir the breadcrumbs, Parmesan, and pesto until well mixed. Top the fennel with the breadcrumb mixture and cook for 5 minutes until lightly browned. Serve.

Honeyed Fry Bread

SERVES 4 ■ PREP TIME: 15 MINUTES, PLUS RESTING TIME ■ COOK TIME: 20 MINUTES

In my current small town in northern Canada, there is a restaurant featuring quite possibly the best food I have ever encountered as a chef and guest. The menu features many dishes inspired by chef Gerry's First Nation heritage, such as fry bread. It is exceptional, and I was delighted to create a version for my air fryer. Traditional fry bread is made with lard and granulated sugar, but I have substituted vegetable shortening and honey, which creates a complex flavor. If you want vegan fry bread, use maple syrup to drizzle on the finished dish.

1 cup all-purpose flour

1¼ teaspoons baking powder

⅛ teaspoon sea salt

1 tablespoon vegetable shortening

¼ cup hot water

Olive oil, for brushing

Honey, for drizzling

1. In a medium bowl, combine the flour, baking powder, and salt until well blended. Add the shortening and use your fingers to rub until the mixture resembles coarse crumbs.
2. Add the water and mix until a smooth dough forms, kneading about 5 to 7 minutes.
3. Cover the bowl and let it stand for 30 minutes.
4. Turn the dough out onto a floured work surface and divide it into 2 equal pieces. Roll each piece out to a 6-inch circle.
5. Preheat on Air Fry at 370°F (190°C) for 3 minutes.
6. Brush the air fryer basket with oil and place one of the dough circles into the basket. Brush the top generously with oil and cook for 5 minutes. Flip and brush the second side with oil and cook 5 more minutes, until puffy and golden. Repeat with the remaining dough.
7. Serve warm, drizzled with honey.

This recipe is inspired by my First Nation neighbors, but this type of dish can be found all over the world. From the Caribbean to Europe to Asia and Africa, fry bread is stuffed, topped, and used to mop up delicious stews and soups.

Main Courses

Here is where we get to the meat—pardon the pun—of the recipes, the main course. As a chef in the '90s, I witnessed the entire kitchen groan whenever a guest ordered a vegetarian meal. This wasn't "real" food; what kind of imbecile didn't want lamb racks and beef tenderloin? So they served whatever veg and starch were available as sides for the carnivore plates and called it a meal. After watching this sacrilege a few times, I quietly took over creating a properly balanced vegetarian or vegan meal because I fell into this dreaded group myself. Soon, that section of the menu for the dining room and events was my territory, and I knew I had won when twenty wedding guests, including the bride, requested the vegetarian option after seeing the first plate come out. Plant-based main courses are vibrant, texture-packed, and redolent with spices, herbs, and lovely flavors. These recipes come from all over the world and turn out spectacular when made in an air fryer.

Crispy Chinese Eggplant with Soy Honey Sauce page 138

Eggplant Paprikash

SERVES 2 ■ PREP TIME: 15 MINUTES ■ COOK TIME: 30 MINUTES

As you may have guessed by the title, this recipe is a Hungarian love song dedicated to paprika, a gorgeous spice commonly used in that country's spectacular cuisine. Paprika is made from ground pods of *Capsicum annuum* peppers and can be found in several different types in the local grocery store. You will see plain paprika, hot, or smoked on the spice shelves; pick up whatever is recommended in your recipe (smoked in this case). The flavors of each are very different and they are not usually interchangeable. Smoked paprika has a lush, rich flavor that is not fiery or overwhelming. It gently melds with the porous eggplant and tart sour cream in this dish, creating a sublime stew perfect for egg noodles or rice.

½ pound (227 g) of eggplant, cut into 1-inch (2 cm) cubes

½ onion, peeled and sliced

1 tablespoon (15 ml) olive oil

1 teaspoon minced garlic

1 (15-ounce/425 g) can crushed tomatoes

2 tablespoons (14 g) smoked paprika

Sea salt

Freshly ground black pepper

¼ cup (60 ml) heavy (whipping) cream

2 tablespoons (30 g) sour cream

1. In a large bowl, toss the eggplant, onion, oil, and garlic, then transfer them to the air fryer basket.
2. Air Fry at 375°F (190°C) for 10 minutes, tossing once or twice, until tender.
3. Transfer the vegetables to a 7-inch (18 cm) round baking pan (3-inches/7.5 cm deep). Stir in the tomatoes and paprika and cook for 20 minutes, stirring halfway through, until the vegetables are very tender and the flavors are blended.
4. Season with salt and pepper and stir in the heavy cream and sour cream, then serve.

Chickpea Ratatouille

SERVES 2 ■ PREP TIME: 10 MINUTES ■ COOK TIME: 30 MINUTES

From *touiller*, meaning "to stir or toss," ratatouille is a French peasant stew bursting with all the bounty of the summer. It can be enjoyed either hot or cold, spooned over pasta or cooked grains, or by itself with a chunk of crusty bread. The chickpeas are not a traditional addition, but they add a hefty amount of fiber and create a filling meal. You can omit them and change up the vegetables and seasonings in this dish. The recipe is designed to use up whatever you have in the refrigerator or the garden, a kitchen-sink cooking experiment that is delicious no matter what you throw in.

½ small eggplant, peeled and cut into 1-inch (2 cm) pieces

1 cup (150 g) halved cherry tomatoes

1 cup (240 g) canned chickpeas, rinsed

1 zucchini, cut into ½-inch (1 cm) pieces

1 yellow bell pepper, cut into ½-inch (1 cm) pieces

1 red onion, cut into ½-inch (1 cm) pieces

2 teaspoons olive oil

1 teaspoon minced garlic

Pinch red pepper flakes

1 tablespoon (4 g) chopped fresh parsley

1 tablespoon (2.5 g) chopped fresh basil

Sea salt

Freshly ground black pepper

1. In a large bowl, toss the eggplant, cherry tomatoes, chickpeas, zucchini, bell pepper, onion, oil, garlic, and red pepper flakes until the vegetables are coated.
2. Transfer the vegetables to a 7-inch (18 cm) round cakepan (3-inches/7.5 cm deep) and Air Fry at 375°F (190°C) for 30 minutes, tossing every 10 minutes, until the vegetables are very tender, and the flavors are blended.
3. Stir in the parsley and basil and season with salt and pepper. Serve.

How to Convert Your Own Recipes to Air Frying

After getting familiar with your air fryer, you might want to make some favorite family recipes in it. Luckily, it is simple to convert most recipes. First, you might have to scale the recipe down to fit the air fryer, which is a confined space. In general, you can reduce the oil by about half or not use any at all depending on the recipe; experiment to see what works best. Reduce the heat by 25 to 30°F (5 to 10°C) and the cooking time by 20 percent. (Some recipes will not work in the air fryer: wet batter drips through, bacon creates too much mess, tender leafy greens blow around, and raw rice and grains do not cook evenly.)

Mujadarra

SERVES 4 ■ PREP TIME: 10 MINUTES ■ COOK TIME: 50 MINUTES

My mother and I enjoyed a version of this simple, popular Middle Eastern dish in Tripoli, Libya, dished out onto flatbread "plates" by a friendly street vendor with a sparkling gold tooth. The rich caramelized onions elevated simple grains and legumes to culinary perfection with no embellishment or garnish needed. The air fryer is not usually used for cooking grains, but it works just fine for a recipe that does not require refinement, and the onions turn out amazing.

2 large sweet onions, halved and thinly sliced

2 tablespoons (30 ml) olive oil

Sea salt

1 cup (200 g) canned lentils, drained and rinsed

1 cup (200 g) cooked brown rice

½ cup (120 ml) vegetable broth

½ teaspoon ground cumin

2 tablespoons (2 g) chopped fresh cilantro

Lime wedges, for serving

1. In a medium bowl, toss the onion and oil until very well coated and season with salt.
2. Preheat on Air Fry at 400°F (200°C) for 3 minutes.
3. Arrange the onions in the air fryer basket and cook for 10 minutes, tossing very well halfway through. Reduce the heat to 360°F (185°C) and cook for 10 minutes, tossing very well halfway through. Finally, reduce the heat to 300°F (150°C) and cook until crispy and golden, tossing every 5 minutes, about 15 minutes. Remove the onions from the basket to a medium bowl.
4. Let the air fryer cool for 10 minutes and wipe it out with a paper towel. Place half the onions, the lentils, rice, broth, and cumin in a 7-inch (18 cm) round baking pan (3-inches/7.5 cm deep) and Air Fry on 360°F (185°C) for 15 minutes, stirring halfway through, until heated through.
5. Serve the lentils and rice topped with the remaining caramelized onions, cilantro, and lime wedges.

Turkish Baked Potato (Kumpir)

SERVES 2 ■ PREP TIME: 10 MINUTES ■ COOK TIME: 40 MINUTES

Baked potatoes are the side of choice in my home, so a main course version is always welcome. When offered a choice of any dinner—and I am a chef, so that range was vast—my father always picks a loaded baked potato. Since he worked over forty years as an expat in the Middle East, "loaded" meant the popular baked potato street food called kumpir. Toppings included the ones in this recipe plus mushrooms, beets, tomatoes, gherkins, corn, bulgur salad, and carrot. Use this recipe as a base and add all your favorites; the potato can never be too stuffed.

2 large russet potatoes

1 teaspoon avocado oil

1 large tomato, chopped

½ cup (100 g) canned lentils, rinsed

½ cup (50 g) sliced black olives

¼ cup (30 g) pickled vegetables

¼ cup (30 g) shredded cheddar cheese

2 tablespoons (12 g) chopped scallion, both white and green parts

2 tablespoons (30 g) sour cream

Sea salt

Freshly ground black pepper

1. Rub the potatoes with oil and pierce them several times with a fork. Place them in the air fryer basket and Air Fry at 400°F (200°C) until fork-tender, about 40 minutes.
2. Cut each baked potato lengthwise, creating a slit, and open it up by pressing on the ends. Use a fork to mash up the flesh in the potatoes, keeping the skin intact. Top the potatoes with the tomato, lentils, olives, pickled vegetables, cheese, scallion, and sour cream.
3. Season with salt and pepper and serve.

Florentine Bulgur Casserole

SERVES 2 ■ PREP TIME: 10 MINUTES ■ COOK TIME: 25 MINUTES

I love all grains; diets eliminating this food group would not last for one meal in my house. Bulgur finds its way into porridge, eggs, pilafs, stews, and, of course, casseroles. This grain has a chewy texture and exceptional nutty taste that is perfect for this cheesy, spinach-packed meal. The baking pan that fits in my air fryer produces the perfect amount for myself and my husband now that the kids have moved out. You can use any other grain in place of the bulgur in the same amount.

1 cup (70 g) sliced white mushrooms

½ sweet onion, chopped

1 tablespoon (15 ml) olive oil

1 teaspoon minced garlic

1 cup (235 ml) whole milk

½ cup (50 g) grated Parmesan cheese

1 tablespoon (8 g) cornstarch

⅛ teaspoon ground nutmeg

2 cups (370 g) cooked bulgur

2 cups (80 g) packed fresh baby spinach

Freshly ground black pepper

1. In a 7-inch (18 cm) round baking pan (3-inches/7.5 cm deep), toss the mushrooms, onion, oil, and garlic until they are coated.
2. Air Fry at 375°F (190°C) for 8 to 10 minutes, tossing once or twice, until tender.
3. Meanwhile, in a small saucepan, combine the milk, Parmesan cheese, cornstarch, and nutmeg and heat over medium heat until thickened and well blended, about 6 minutes.
4. Stir the sauce, bulgur, and spinach into the mushroom mixture and air fry 15 minutes to heat through.
5. Season with pepper and serve.

Pumpkin Lentil Curry

SERVES 2 ■ PREP TIME: 10 MINUTES ■ COOK TIME: 45 MINUTES

If I only cooked for myself, there is a good chance some sort of curry would be on my table at least three or four times a week. I am obsessed with this dish, and this variation comes from my time as a chef in Tripoli when I learned all about green and red curries from our dish washer's mother. Pumpkin is a common ingredient in stews in this region, and it is lovely in curry along with the lentils and pretty green kale. I use red curry paste in this dish and sometimes a half cup of coconut milk when I want a creamier, more saucy stew. You can find frozen pumpkin in most stores, but you will have to thaw it and cut the chunks smaller so it cooks quicker in the air fryer.

2 cups (340 g) pumpkin cubes (½ inch/1 cm)

½ cup (80 g) chopped sweet onion

1 tablespoon (15 ml) olive oil

½ cup (120 ml) low-sodium vegetable broth

½ cup (120 ml) coconut milk

1 tablespoon mild or hot curry powder (7 g) or paste (15 g)

1 teaspoon peeled and grated ginger

½ teaspoon minced garlic

1 cup (200 g) canned lentils, rinsed and drained

1 cup (67 g) shredded kale

1. In a medium bowl, toss the pumpkin, onion, and oil until well coated.
2. Transfer to the air fryer basket and Air Fry at 375°F (190°C) for 15 to 18 minutes, tossing once or twice, until tender.
3. While the pumpkin is cooking, in a medium saucepan, heat the broth, coconut milk, curry, ginger, and garlic on medium-high heat until just simmering, about 6 minutes.
4. Transfer the pumpkin mixture to a 7-inch (18 cm) round baking pan (3-inches/7.5 cm deep) and stir in the lentils, kale, and curry sauce. Cook for 25 minutes until heated through.
5. Serve over rice or with naan.

Tofu Buffalo "Wings" with Blue Cheese Dip

SERVES 4 ■ PREP TIME: 15 MINUTES ■ COOK TIME: 20 MINUTES

Before you ask, this dish does not taste like chicken. Although I appreciate the quality of many vegetarian and vegan products designed to be meat alternatives, I prefer enjoying plant-based foods for their own wonderful textures and flavors. That said, I love the combination of wing hot sauce and blue cheese, and these crispy tofu sticks provide the ideal base to indulge that craving without meat. Air fryer tofu sticks have enough texture and crispy edges to hold up when tossed with the sauce, and the light breading soaks up all that fiery flavor. The blue cheese dip is delicious with cut vegetables, so double the batch for another snack.

1. Place the cornstarch, milk, and breadcrumbs in 3 small bowls.
2. Dredge each tofu wing in the cornstarch, then milk, and then breadcrumbs until well coated.
3. Preheat on Air Fry at 400°F (200°C) for 3 minutes. Lightly spray the air fryer basket with oil.
4. Working in batches, place the tofu wings in a single layer in the basket, lightly spray them with oil, and cook for 10 minutes, shaking halfway through, until golden and crispy. Repeat with the remaining tofu.
5. While the tofu is cooking, mix together the blue cheese, buttermilk, sour cream, mayonnaise, and lime juice in a medium bowl until combined. Season with salt and pepper and refrigerate in a covered container until serving.
6. When the tofu is almost done cooking, mix the hot sauce and butter in a medium bowl until blended. Add the crispy tofu wings to the bowl and toss to coat.
7. Serve with the blue cheese dipping sauce.

Tofu Buffalo "Wings"

½ cup (64 g) cornstarch

½ cup (120 ml) coconut milk

1 cup (115 g) panko breadcrumbs

1 (14-ounce/400 g) block extra-firm tofu, pressed (see page 30) and cut into 1x3-inch (2.5x75 cm) sticks

Oil spray

½ cup (120 ml) hot sauce

3 tablespoons (42 g) melted butter

Blue Cheese Dip

¾ cup (90 g) blue cheese crumbles

¼ cup (60 ml) buttermilk

¼ cup (60 g) sour cream

¼ cup (60 g) mayonnaise

Juice of 1 lime

Sea salt

Freshly ground black pepper

North African Tagine

SERVES 4 ■ PREP TIME: 10 MINUTES ■ COOK TIME: 55 MINUTES

My years spent cooking my way through North Africa produced a passion for spices and an admiration for a humble cooking vessel called a tagine. This conical ceramic or clay pot comes in various sizes and can hold single portions or enough for a whole family. Over time, the word *tagine* came to describe the dish rather than the vessel and referred to any spice-laced, stew-like recipe cooked in a moist, sealed environment. Placing a covered pan in the air fryer basket creates this environment, and not a single drop of flavor is lost. I learned the taste combinations on show here, such as tomatoes, sweet potatoes, apricots, ginger, citrus, and bright parsley, in Tunisia, Libya, and Morocco. Try it over a bed of fluffy basmati rice or warm flatbread to soak up all the sauce.

2 cups (260 g) cauliflower florets

1 carrot, shredded

½ small sweet potato, cut into ¼-inch (5 mm) pieces

½ cup (80 g) chopped sweet onion

1 tablespoon (15 ml) olive oil

1 (15-ounce/425 g) can sodium-free diced tomatoes

¼ cup (44 g) dried apricots, chopped

1 teaspoon peeled and grated fresh ginger

1 teaspoon minced garlic

1 teaspoon ground cumin

½ teaspoon ground cinnamon

Juice of ½ lemon

1 tablespoon (4 g) chopped fresh parsley

1. Preheat on Air Fry at 375°F (190°C) for 3 minutes.
2. Toss the cauliflower, carrot, sweet potato, onion, and oil together in the air fryer basket. Cook until the vegetables are tender, about 20 to 25 minutes, stirring at least twice.
3. In a medium saucepan, heat the tomatoes, apricot, ginger, garlic, cumin, and cinnamon until just simmering.
4. Transfer the vegetables to a 7-inch (18 cm) round baking pan (3-inches/7.5 cm deep) and stir in the tomato mixture until well mixed. Cover tightly with aluminum foil and cook for 25 minutes until the flavors mellow.
5. Uncover and cook 5 minutes more.
6. Stir in the lemon juice and serve topped with parsley.

Summer Squash Rigatoni Bake

SERVES 2 ■ PREP TIME: 10 MINUTES ■ COOK TIME: 30 MINUTES

Baked pasta is a traditional comfort food, from lasagna to cannelloni to the mac and cheese in this book (Quattro Formaggi Macaroni, page 144). This recipe is less cheesy and features piles of summer vegetables, perfect for a leisurely meal with a fresh green salad. You might be wondering whether summer squash is the same thing as zucchini, and the short answer is that they are both summer squash, as opposed to thick-skinned golden winter squash. In this case, summer squash is the bright yellow one, usually sitting next to the green zucchini in the produce section. You can use all green if nothing else is available.

2 yellow summer squash, quartered lengthwise and sliced

1 green zucchini, quartered lengthwise and sliced

½ red onion, chopped

1 tablespoon (15 ml) olive oil

1 teaspoon minced garlic

1 large tomato, chopped

½ cup (125 g) ricotta cheese

1 large egg, beaten

2 tablespoons (5 g) chopped fresh basil

Pinch red pepper flakes

3 cups (420 g) cooked rigatoni

¼ cup (20 g) shredded Parmesan cheese

1. In a medium bowl, toss the summer squash, zucchini, onion, oil, and garlic until the vegetables are well coated. Transfer them to a 7-inch (18 cm) round baking pan (3-inches/7.5 cm deep) and Air Fry at 375°F (190°C) for 8 to 10 minutes, tossing once or twice, until tender.
2. Stir in the tomato, ricotta cheese, egg, basil, and red pepper flakes and cook 15 minutes, stirring halfway through.
3. Stir in the rigatoni and top with Parmesan cheese. Air fry for 5 minutes until the cheese is melted and serve.

Chard and Gruyere Panade

SERVES 4 ■ PREP TIME: 15 MINUTES ■ COOK TIME: 38 MINUTES

What is a panade, you might ask? It is bread soaked in broth, combined with vegetables or other ingredients, and baked until the texture is almost velvety. Unlike its culinary cousin bread pudding, a panade has no eggs or cream. This version is packed with healthy dark leafy greens, onion, thyme, and tempting gruyere cheese. The air fryer creates a gorgeous crunchy browned crust that you might be tempted to eat before the rest of the dish.

1 tablespoon (15 ml) olive oil, plus extra for greasing

1 small sweet onion, chopped

2 teaspoons minced garlic

3 cups (108 g) chopped Swiss chard

1 teaspoon chopped fresh thyme

¼ teaspoon ground nutmeg

3 cups (200 g) French bread, cut into ½-inch (1 cm) cubes

1 cup (120 g) shredded gruyere cheese, divided

Sea salt

Freshly ground black pepper

2 cups (475 ml) low-sodium vegetable broth

1. Lightly grease a 7-inch (18 cm) round baking pan (3-inches/7.5 cm deep).
2. Heat the oil in a medium skillet over medium-high heat. Sauté the onion and garlic until softened, about 3 minutes. Add the chard and sauté until wilted, about 5 minutes. Add the thyme and nutmeg and toss.
3. Remove from the heat and add the bread cubes and half the cheese, stirring until well mixed. Season with salt and pepper and transfer the mixture to the prepared pan.
4. Preheat the air fryer on Roast at 350°F (180°C) for 3 minutes.
5. While the air fryer is preheating, bring the broth to a boil in a small saucepan over high heat.
6. Pour the broth over the bread mixture. stirring so it soaks in well. Cover with foil and cook for 20 minutes.
7. Remove the foil, top with the remaining cheese, and cook for 10 minutes until golden and the cheese is melted. Serve.

Sauerkraut Colcannon

SERVES 4 ■ PREP TIME: 10 MINUTES ■ COOK TIME: 40 MINUTES

My mother could make the most incredible Indonesian food, but her regular culinary repertoire was limited to about ten recipes. When my parents were married, for the first five months, she served a version of this dish almost every night to my bemused father, because it was the only "North American" dish she knew how to make. Of course, it really isn't really a dish from that area—it's actually Irish in origin—but he ate it anyway to please her, every night. This version is close to the one I made with my mom, except we obviously did not have an air fryer in those days. I still have a hard time not picking off the crunchy golden crust from the top when it comes out. It is hands-down the best part.

2 large russet potatoes, peeled and cut into 1-inch (2 cm) pieces

½ sweet onion, sliced thinly

1 tablespoon (15 ml) olive oil

2 teaspoons minced garlic

¼ cup (60 ml) coconut milk

Sea salt

Freshly ground black pepper

2 cups (285 g) bottled or canned sauerkraut

2 tablespoons (8 g) chopped fresh parsley

1. Place the potatoes in a medium saucepan and cover them with 2 inches (5 cm) of water. Bring the water to a boil over high heat, reduce the heat to medium-low, and simmer the potatoes until tender, about 15 minutes.
2. While the potatoes are cooking, toss the onion, oil, and garlic in a 7-inch (18 cm) round baking pan (3-inches/7.5 cm deep) until coated. Air Fry at 375°F (190°C) for 5 to 6 minutes, tossing once or twice, until tender.
3. Drain the potatoes, mash them with the coconut milk, and season with salt and pepper.
4. Stir the potatoes into the onions with the sauerkraut and parsley.
5. Cook until heated through and the top is lightly browned, about 20 minutes. Serve hot.

Kale Spanakopita Pie

SERVES 4 ■ PREP TIME: 20 MINUTES ■ COOK TIME: 20 MINUTES

Over the years, in many different kitchens, I have folded and folded (and folded) little spanakopita triangles in the hundreds for countless weddings and corporate events. This traditional appetizer is a fan favorite, so creating an easy-to-prepare pie using the same flavors was a no-brainer. Phyllo cooks up beautifully in the air fryer; this ingredient seems made for that cooking environment. Don't worry if the completed dish looks a little rustic with all the tucked and folded edges; it tastes delicious.

6 ounces (170 g) frozen chopped kale, thawed and squeezed out

¼ sweet onion, chopped

1 scallion, white and green parts, chopped

1 tablespoon (4 g) chopped fresh parsley

1 tablespoon (6 g) chopped fresh mint

1 tablespoon (15 ml) freshly squeezed lemon juice

½ teaspoon minced garlic

¾ cup (112 g) crumbled feta cheese

1 large egg, beaten

¼ teaspoon ground nutmeg

10 sheets phyllo pastry, cut in half

¼ cup (55 g) melted butter

1. In a medium bowl, stir the kale, onion, scallion, parsley, mint, lemon juice, garlic, feta, egg, and nutmeg until well combined.
2. Place the phyllo sheets on a clean work surface and cover them with a clean, damp kitchen cloth.
3. Lightly grease a 7-inch (18 cm) round baking pan with butter. Place 2 sheets of phyllo in the dish, pressing them into the bottom edges. They can drape up the sides a little. Brush the top sheet with butter. Repeat until you have 10 stacked sheets.
4. Add the filling to the pan and spread it evenly over the phyllo. Layer the remaining 10 sheets, 2 at a time, brushing the top sheet with butter, until you have 10 sheets layered on the top. Trim the edges or tuck them in so there is no excess hanging over the sides. Score the top into quarters, cutting about 6 sheets into the top.
5. Preheat on Air Fry at 390°F (195°C) for 3 minutes.
6. Cook for 20 to 22 minutes until crispy and golden.
7. Let cool for 10 minutes, cut the pie into quarters, and serve.

Use any dark leafy green in place of the kale, such as spinach, the classic choice, or Swiss chard, or even a combination of greens.

Swedish "Meatballs"

SERVES 4 ■ PREP TIME: 15 MINUTES, PLUS CHILLING TIME ■ COOK TIME: 25 MINUTES

Meatballs are one of those foods that crop up in many dishes, from appetizers to main courses, in all types of sauces, and created with a plethora of ingredients. The "meatballs" in creamy mustard sauce here are lentil-based and accented with parmesan cheese, garlic, and herbs. You can also whip them up in the air fryer to use in a tomato sauce for spaghetti, as a pita stuffing, or glazed in a sweet and sour sauce for a tempting appetizer.

Meatballs

1 teaspoon olive oil

¼ small onion, finely chopped

2 teaspoons minced garlic

1 (15-ounce/425 g) can low-sodium lentils, drained and rinsed

½ cup (40 g) shredded Parmesan cheese

1 large egg

2 tablespoons (8 g) chopped fresh parsley

1 tablespoon (8 g) all-purpose flour

Sea salt

Oil spray

Sauce

3 tablespoons (42 g) butter

3 tablespoons (24 g) all-purpose flour

1½ cups (255 ml) vegetable stock

2 teaspoons Worcestershire sauce

2 teaspoons Dijon mustard

¾ cup (175 ml) heavy (whipping) cream

Sea salt

Freshly ground black pepper

1. Heat the oil in a small skillet over medium-high heat. Sauté the onion and garlic until softened, about 2 minutes. Transfer them to a food processor and add the lentils, Parmesan cheese, egg, parsley, and flour and pulse until just combined and the mixture holds together when pressed.
2. Roll the lentil mixture into 1½-inch (3 cm) meatballs, about 18 in total. Place in the refrigerator for 15 minutes to firm up.
3. Preheat at Air Fry at 390°F (195°C) for 3 minutes. Lightly spray the air fryer basket with oil.
4. Working in batches if necessary, place the meatballs in a single layer in the basket and spray them with oil. Cook for 12 minutes until heated throughout and lightly browned, turning halfway through. Repeat with the remaining meatballs and keep the cooked ones warm on a plate loosely covered with foil.
5. While the meatballs are cooking, melt the butter in a medium saucepan over medium-high heat.
6. Whisk in the flour until a thick paste forms and the flour cooks out, about 2 minutes. Add the stock, Worcestershire sauce, and Dijon mustard and whisk until the sauce is smooth and thick, about 2 minutes.
7. Remove from the heat, whisk in the cream, and season with salt and pepper.
8. In a large bowl, toss the meatballs with the sauce and serve with rice, egg noodles, or vegetable noodles.

Sweet Potato Bean Enchiladas

SERVES 3 ■ PREP TIME: 15 MINUTES ■ COOK TIME: 22 MINUTES

The lightly spiced sweet potato base for these gorgeous enchiladas is created in the air fryer first, so the veggies are tender and rich. Then all the other ingredients are stirred in to create a cheesy, bean-laden, spicy casserole that will delight your taste buds. Combining everything rather than rolling the fillings into the tortillas means this dish takes less time. If you want a more finished, rolled dish, you can create full enchiladas, top with the sauce and cheese, and air fry it that way instead.

2 sweet potatoes, peeled and cut into ½-inch (1 cm) cubes

1 small sweet onion, cut into eighths

1 tablespoon (15 ml) olive oil

1 teaspoon ground cumin

½ teaspoon chili powder

1 cup (175 g) black beans, drained and rinsed

1 jalapeño, chopped

1(15-ounce/425 g) can red enchilada sauce

4 corn tortillas, cut into ½-inch (1 cm) strips

1 cup (115 g) shredded Mexican cheese

1 tablespoon (1 g) chopped fresh cilantro

1. Preheat on Air Fry at 400°F (200°C) for 3 minutes.
2. In a medium bowl, toss the sweet potato, onion, oil, cumin, and chili powder until well coated.
3. Transfer the mixture to a 7-inch (18 cm) round baking pan. Cook for 12 minutes, tossing halfway through, until tender.
4. Stir in the beans, jalapeño, enchilada sauce, and tortillas until well mixed. Top with the cheese and cook until the cheese is melted, and the mixture is bubbly, about 10 minutes.
5. Serve topped with cilantro.

Bell Pepper Stuffed with Pelau (Coconut Rice)

SERVES 4 ■ PREP TIME: 10 MINUTES ■ COOK TIME: 42 MINUTES

I was never a fan of stuffed peppers as a child; I actually hid under my bed once for two hours to avoid them. Eventually, I discovered that it wasn't the peppers I detested; it was my mother's overcooked bland preparation, bless her heart. Peppers are the ideal container for this slightly spicy Caribbean coconut rice because the sweetness pairs beautifully. The splash of citrus, chopped cashews, and glorious green cilantro elevate this dish beyond a simple family meal to a restaurant-quality experience.

1 teaspoon extra-virgin olive oil

1 large carrot, shredded

½ sweet onion, finely chopped

1 tablespoon (10 g) minced jalapeño pepper

1 teaspoon minced garlic

½ teaspoon peeled and grated ginger

2 cups (475 ml) canned coconut milk

1½ cups (293 g) uncooked white rice

1 cup (235 ml) water

1 tablespoon (15 g) brown sugar

Sea salt

¼ cup (34 g) chopped cashews

Juice of 1 lemon

1 tablespoon (1 g) chopped fresh cilantro

4 bell peppers, tops cut off and seeded

1. Heat the oil in a large saucepan over medium-high heat. Sauté the carrot, onion, jalapeño, garlic, and ginger until softened, about 4 minutes.
2. Add the coconut milk, rice, water, and brown sugar, stir, and bring to a boil. Cover, reduce the heat to low, and simmer until the liquid is absorbed and the rice is tender, about 20 minutes.
3. Season with salt and stir in the cashews, lemon juice, and cilantro. Evenly divide the rice among the peppers.
4. Preheat on Air Fry at 360°F (185°C) for 3 minutes. Place the stuffed peppers in the air fryer basket and cook until the peppers are very tender, about 15 to 18 minutes. Serve.

Any vegetables can be stuffed with this delicious rice, such as tomatoes, zucchini, or acorn squash. The softer vegetables can be completed in the same cooking time but if using winter squash, cook the vegetable for 20 minutes first before stuffing and cooking for an additional 15 minutes.

Baked Chipotle Chili with Cheddar and Tortilla Chips

SERVES 4 ■ PREP TIME: 10 MINUTES ■ COOK TIME: 55 MINUTES

Chili is an incredibly versatile dish. It can be a main course or a tempting topping for nachos and veggie dogs. This version comes together well in the air fryer, and the leftovers taste even better the second day. My favorite way to eat this thick, spicy recipe is topped with sharp cheddar and crunchy tortilla chips. The different textures are delightful, and if you add a dollop of sour cream, your taste buds will thank you.

1 cup (256 g) kidney beans, rinsed and drained

1 cup (192 g) lentils, rinsed and drained

1 (15-ounce/425 g) can diced tomatoes and their juices

½ small sweet onion, finely diced

1 small red bell pepper, chopped

1 small green bell pepper, chopped

½ jalapeño pepper, seeded and finely diced

1 teaspoon minced garlic

1 teaspoon chipotle chili powder

½ teaspoon ground cumin

¼ teaspoon ground coriander

⅛ teaspoon cayenne pepper (optional)

½ cup (60 g) shredded cheddar cheese, for garnish

10 tortilla chips, broken into small pieces, for garnish

1. In a large bowl, combine the kidney beans, lentils, diced tomatoes, onion, bell peppers, jalapeño pepper, garlic, chili powder, cumin, coriander, and cayenne pepper (if using) until well mixed.
2. Transfer the mixture to a 7-inch (18 cm) round baking pan (3-inches/7.5 cm deep) and cover tightly with foil. Poke a couple holes in the foil with a skewer.
3. Cook the chili in the air fryer on Roast at 390°F (195°C) for 50 minutes, stirring every 20 minutes, until the vegetables are tender and the chili is piping hot. Remove the foil and cook 5 minutes longer.
4. Serve topped with cheddar and tortillas.

Crispy Chinese Eggplant with Soy Honey Sauce

SERVES 2 ■ PREP TIME: 15 MINUTES ■ COOK TIME: 20 MINUTES

Eggplant is a typical ingredient in Chinese cuisine, although the variety used is different from the large vegetables common to Mediterranean and North African cuisine. Chinese eggplant is smaller, has fewer seeds, and does not have the bitter taste of its larger counterpart. If you can find the smaller one in your grocery store or market, please use it in this recipe. The combination of crispy vegetables and the spectacular sauce in this dish is a culinary masterpiece, especially when spooned over fluffy basmati rice.

1 medium eggplant, cut into 1-inch (2 cm) pieces

2 tablespoons (30 ml) olive oil

1 tablespoon (15 ml) sesame oil

2 scallions, white and green parts, sliced thinly on a bias

2 teaspoons minced garlic

2 teaspoons peeled and grated fresh ginger

¼ cup (60 ml) low-sodium soy sauce

2 tablespoons (30 ml) rice wine vinegar

2 tablespoons (60 g) honey

Pinch red pepper flakes

2 tablespoons (30 ml) water

1 teaspoon cornstarch

1 tablespoon (8 g) sesame seeds

1. In a medium bowl, toss the eggplant with the olive oil until well coated.
2. Preheat on Air Fry at 375°F (190°C) for 3 minutes.
3. Place the eggplant in the air fryer basket and cook until very crispy and golden, for about 20 to 22 minutes, tossing halfway through.
4. While the eggplant is cooking, heat the sesame oil in a large skillet over medium heat and sauté the scallions, garlic, and ginger for 2 minutes.
5. Add the soy sauce, vinegar, honey, and red pepper flakes and cook for 2 minutes.
6. In a small bowl, stir the water and cornstarch until a smooth paste forms. Add the mixture to the skillet and stir until the sauce thickens, about 30 seconds. Remove the skillet from the heat until the eggplant is done.
7. Add the crispy eggplant to the skillet and toss to coat with the sauce. Sprinkle with sesame seeds and serve.

Cabbage Scallion Strudel

SERVES 4 ■ PREP TIME: 15 MINUTES ■ COOK TIME: 15 MINUTES

You might be reminded of Scandinavian dishes when you first try this simple strudel: clean flavors, minimalistic presentation, and, of course, caraway seeds. The cabbage needs to be very finely shredded for the texture to be right, so don't cut corners and throw in a store-bought coleslaw mix. The filling should be tender but with a little bite similar to perfectly cooked pasta. If you prefer a softer version, sauté the cabbage and scallions first in a little oil until the desired consistency, squeeze the liquid out, and add the vegetables to the other filling ingredients.

6 sheets phyllo pastry

½ small green cabbage, finely shredded

2 scallions, white and green parts, chopped

½ cup (115 g) Greek yogurt

¼ cup (60 g) sour cream

¼ teaspoon caraway seeds (optional)

Sea salt

Freshly ground black pepper

Melted butter, for brushing

1. Lay a sheet of phyllo on a clean work surface and brush it lightly with butter. Stack the remaining sheets on top, brushing each with butter before laying the next on top. Fit the prepared sheets in a 7-inch (18 cm) round baking pan, pressing the bottom and sides flat and draping the excess evenly over the edges.
2. In a large bowl, toss the cabbage, scallions, yogurt, sour cream, and caraway seeds (if using) until well mixed. Season with salt and pepper.
3. Place the cabbage filling in the phyllo-covered baking pan and fold the edges over the filling in a package. Brush the edges and top generously with melted butter.
4. Preheat on Air Fry at 390°F (195°C) for 3 minutes.
5. Cook the strudel for 15 minutes, or until golden brown and the filling is tender.
6. Let the strudel cool for 10 minutes and then remove it from the pan, cut, and serve.

Southern Fried Cauliflower

SERVES 2 ■ PREP TIME: 10 MINUTES ■ COOK TIME: 20 MINUTES

The secret recipe of a famous restaurant chain claims to use eleven herbs and spices to produce its signature flavor. This dish uses nine, and the taste is equally spectacular. Cauliflower is one of those ingredients made for an air fryer. Its tightly bunched florets have crevices to hold the breading, and cauliflower cooks up crispy and tender, but still firm enough for a satisfying bite. These are stellar with a favorite dipping sauce or a spoonful of marinara on a bed of rice for the main meal. You might just finish them directly from the air fryer basket with your fingers while deciding the serving options.

½ cup (63 g) all-purpose flour

1 teaspoon paprika

½ teaspoon garlic powder

½ teaspoon ground ginger

½ teaspoon onion powder

½ teaspoon mustard powder

½ teaspoon dried thyme

½ teaspoon celery salt

½ teaspoon sea salt

¼ teaspoon freshly ground black pepper

1 cup (235 ml) whole milk

1 cup (110 g) panko breadcrumbs

1 small head cauliflower, cut into medium florets

Oil spray

1. In a large bowl, mix together the flour, paprika, garlic powder, ginger, onion powder, mustard powder, thyme, celery salt, salt, and pepper until blended. Place the bowl on your work surface. Place the milk in another large bowl, and the breadcrumbs in a third large bowl.
2. Add the cauliflower florets to the flour mixture and toss until they are completely coated.
3. Dredge each floret in the milk and then in the breadcrumbs. Place the breaded florets on a cutting board and repeat until all are breaded.
4. Preheat on Air Fry at 350°F (180°C) for 3 minutes. Lightly spray the air fryer basket with oil.
5. Working in batches if necessary, lightly spray the florets, place them in a single layer in the basket, and cook for 10 minutes, tossing halfway through, until golden and crispy.
6. Repeat with the remaining cauliflower and serve.

Homity Pie (Potato Leek Pie)

SERVES 2 ■ PREP TIME: 15 MINUTES ■ COOK TIME: 35 MINUTES

This is a backward homity pie, but it will taste the same. The traditional pie is an open-faced vegetable creation rather than covered with the crust, and this version uses puff pastry instead of a standard pie pastry. Despite all these differences, the dish's essence is present: leeks, potatoes, and onions in a thick, creamy sauce. You can undoubtedly construct the pie with a regular pie crust on the bottom and filling on the top, but then you will miss the tempting moment when the fragrant, herb-infused steam escapes from the first cut. Whatever way you make this dish, it will be a comforting, filling meal for a chilly day.

3 russet potatoes, peeled and cut into ½-inch (1 cm) cubes

1 large carrot, peeled and cut into ¼-inch (5 mm) pieces

3 tablespoons (42 g) butter

1 large leek, white and light green parts, washed and sliced

1 teaspoon minced garlic

½ teaspoon chopped fresh thyme

3 tablespoons (24 g) all-purpose flour

1 cup (235 ml) vegetable stock

½ cup (120 ml) heavy (whipping) cream

Sea salt

Freshly ground black pepper

1 sheet puff pastry

1 large egg, beaten

1. Bring a large saucepan filled three-quarters full of water to a boil over medium-high heat. Add the potatoes and carrots and boil until tender, about 10 minutes. Drain and transfer the vegetables to a small bowl.
2. Place the saucepan back over medium-high heat and melt the butter. Add the leeks, garlic, and thyme and sauté until tender, about 5 minutes. Add the flour and stir for 3 minutes to form a paste and cook the flour. Whisk in the stock until the sauce is very thick, about 3 minutes. Remove from the heat, whisk in the cream, and season with salt and pepper. Add the potatoes and carrots, stirring to coat.
3. Transfer the mixture to a 7-inch (18 cm) round baking pan.
4. Lay the puff pastry on a clean work surface and cut it out to be an 8-inch (20 cm) round. Place the puff pastry over the filling and let the edges hang over the sides, pinching along the edge to seal.
5. Brush the puff pastry with the beaten egg and cut four slits in the top.
6. Preheat on Air Fry at 375°F (190°C) for 3 minutes.
7. Cook pie for 15 minutes, or until golden brown and the filling is bubbly. Serve.

Quattro Formaggi Macaroni

SERVES 3 ■ PREP TIME: 10 MINUTES ■ COOK TIME: 50 MINUTES

For years, mac and cheese was prepared every single day in my home from packages using neon-orange "cheese" powder; I had two growing teenage boys, enough said. They have since moved their 6'4" selves out of my house, carting at least twenty boxes of pasta with them, and I can indulge myself with real four-cheese macaroni. You will have to make the sauce on the stove, but the elbow noodles cook from dry in this delectable cheesy liquid in the air fryer, no boiling necessary. For a tasty finish, mix ½ cup (60 g) of seasoned breadcrumbs with 2 tablespoons (28 g) of melted butter and top the finished pasta with the mixture. Place the uncovered pan back in the air fryer and cook until golden, about 3 minutes.

3 tablespoons (42 g) butter

¼ small onion, finely chopped

½ teaspoon minced garlic

1½ cups (355 ml) whole milk

1½ cups (355 ml) chicken stock

⅓ cup (77 g) cream cheese

8 ounces (228 g) dry elbow macaroni

¾ cup (86 g) shredded cheddar cheese

¾ cup (86 g) shredded mozzarella cheese

½ cup (55 g) shredded fontina cheese

¼ teaspoon ground nutmeg

Sea salt

Freshly ground black pepper

1. Melt the butter in a medium saucepan over medium-high heat. Sauté the onion and garlic until softened, about 2 minutes. Add the milk, chicken stock, and cream cheese and heat, stirring, until the cheese is melted, and the liquid is hot but not boiling.
2. In a medium bowl, mix the hot liquid, pasta, cheddar, mozzarella, fontina, and nutmeg until well combined. Season with salt and pepper.
3. Transfer the mixture to a 7-inch (18 cm) round baking pan (3-inch/7.5 cm deep) and cover tightly with foil.
4. Preheat on Air Fry at 400°F (200°C) for 3 minutes.
5. Cook for 45 minutes, stirring about halfway through, until the pasta is tender, and the mixture is thick and creamy.
6. Serve as written, or topped with breadcrumbs.

Sesame Fried Rice

SERVES 2 ■ PREP TIME: 10 MINUTES ■ COOK TIME: 18 MINUTES

Fried rice is one of the most ordered dishes on Chinese restaurant menus in Western countries, and for good reason. You can add anything to it and have a tasty meal. Making fried rice in an air fryer is simple, and the rice turns out basically identical to restaurant versions. Stirring the rice to expose all the grains to the hot air creates the signature crispy grains in the "real" dish.

2 cups (330 g) cooked white rice

2 teaspoons sesame oil

2 teaspoons low-sodium soy sauce

1 teaspoon canola oil

½ teaspoon minced garlic

½ teaspoon peeled and grated fresh ginger

1 large egg, beaten

¾ cup (98 g) frozen stir-fry vegetables, thawed

1 scallion, green part only, chopped

1 teaspoon sesame seeds

1. Preheat on Air Fry at 350°F (180°C) for 3 minutes.
2. In a medium bowl, toss the rice, sesame oil, soy sauce, canola oil, garlic, and ginger until well mixed. Transfer the mixture to a 7-inch (18 cm) round baking pan.
3. Cook for 10 minutes, stirring halfway through, until the rice is lightly toasted.
4. Pour the beaten egg on top of the rice and cook until it is set, about 3 minutes. Stir the vegetables into the rice, breaking up the cooked egg at the same time, and cook until heated through, 4 to 5 minutes.
5. Serve topped with scallions and sesame seeds.

Zucchini Rice Fritters

SERVES 4 ■ PREP TIME: 10 MINUTES ■ COOK TIME: 20 MINUTES

Turn leftover rice—whether homemade or takeout—into a satisfying vegetarian meal by adding fresh vegetables, herbs, and basic pantry ingredients and make a delicious fritter that cooks up brown and crispy in the air fryer. With zucchini, mint, and lemon, these rice fritters take their flavor inspiration from the Greek Isles. A little grated cheese makes them oh-so-gooey and nearly irresistible even for picky eaters.

The only binder for these fritters is beaten egg, so it is important that you firmly pack the rice mixture into a ball before dredging it in the breadcrumbs. If you are having trouble getting your rice fritters to hold together, try chilling them for 15 minutes after forming.

3 cups (495 g) cooked rice

2 cups (240 g) grated cheese, such as cheddar, Swiss, or gruyere

1 medium zucchini, grated (about 2 cups)

4 scallions, white and light green parts only, sliced

¼ cup (24 g) tightly packed chopped fresh mint

3 eggs, beaten

Kosher salt

Freshly ground black pepper

1¼ cups (83 g) panko breadcrumbs

Oil spray

Lemon wedges, for serving

1. Combine the cooked rice, grated cheese, grated zucchini, scallions, and mint in a large bowl. Add the beaten eggs and season with salt and pepper. Stir to combine, making sure the egg is evenly distributed through the rice.
2. Spread the panko on a plate. Scoop out approximately ½ cup (82.5 g) of the rice mixture and form into a ball with your hands, pressing firmly to make the fritters as tight and well-packed as possible. Dredge the ball in the panko. Repeat with the remaining rice mixture. You should be able to make 8 or 9 fritters. Place half the fritters on a plate and chill until needed.
3. Spray the remaining half of the rice fritters and the basket of the air fryer with oil to prevent sticking. Place the fritters in the basket of the air fryer and cook Air Fry at 400°F (200°C) until browned on all sides and cooked through, 10 to 12 minutes. Carefully remove the fritters to a platter, place the remaining fritters in the air fryer, and cook in the same manner. Serve the rice fritters with lemon wedges for spritzing.

Falafel with Israeli Salad

SERVES 4 ■ PREP TIME: 25 MINUTES, PLUS SOAKING AND RESTING TIME ■ COOK TIME: 30 MINUTES

It is surprisingly easy to make crispy, herbaceous falafel at home, especially if you can cook them in an air fryer as opposed to deep-frying. For best results, however, you must start with softened, but not cooked, dried chickpeas. Canned chickpeas are too soft to form the coarse-ground texture needed for falafel. To soften dry chickpeas, you can soak them overnight or—if planning ahead is not your strong suit—you can boil them quickly and then soak them for just an hour.

It would be most traditional to serve these falafel with Tahini Sauce (page 149), but if you do not care for tahini, or if, like me, someone in your family is allergic to sesame, either tzatziki or toum would make a delicious accompaniment.

Falafel

8 ounces (225 g) dried chickpeas

1 cup (60 g) fresh flat-leaf or Italian parsley, lightly packed

3 cloves garlic

3 scallions, white and light green parts only

1 teaspoon kosher salt

1 teaspoon cumin

½ teaspoon coriander

Pinch cayenne pepper

Juice of ½ lemon

Oil spray

Israeli Salad

2 red bell peppers, chopped

1 English or hothouse cucumber, thickly sliced and quartered

1 small red onion, diced

3 tablespoons (45 ml) extra-virgin olive oil

2 tablespoons (30 ml) red wine vinegar

1 teaspoon kosher salt

Freshly ground black pepper

1. Soak the dried chickpeas in 10 cups (2.4 L) of water overnight and drain. Or, combine the chickpeas and 10 cups (2.4 L) of water in a large saucepan. Bring to a boil over high heat and boil for 2 minutes. Remove from the heat, cover, and allow to sit for at least 1 hour. Drain the chickpeas.

2. Combine the soaked and drained chickpeas, parsley, garlic, scallions, salt, spices, and lemon juice in a food processor. Pulse, scraping down the sides as necessary, until the chickpeas are finely minced but not puréed, and the mixture resembles small grains of cous-cous. When you gather a small amount of the mixture in your hand and squeeze, it should hold together. Scoop ¼ cup (64 g) of the chickpea mixture and form into a tight ball or oval with your hands. Place the chickpea patty on a plate. Repeat with the remaining mixture. You should be able to form 12 balls. Chill for at least 15 minutes.

3. While the chickpea patties are chilling, make the Israeli salad. Combine the red peppers, cucumber, and red onion in a medium bowl. Drizzle the olive oil and vinegar over the vegetables and season with salt and pepper. Toss to combine. Cover and refrigerate the salad while you cook the falafel.

4. To cook the falafel, spray the air fryer basket with oil. Place half the falafel patties in the basket and spray the tops with oil. Air Fry at 400°F (200°C) until the tops are browned and crisp, about 8 minutes. Flip the falafel and spray the second side with oil. Cook until the second side is browned, 5 to 7 additional minutes. Remove the falafel and repeat with the remaining patties.

5. Serve the falafel with the Israeli salad on the side.

Mombasa Masala Chips

SERVES 2–4 ■ PREP TIME: 30 MINUTES, PLUS SOAKING TIME ■ COOK TIME: 25 MINUTES

Looking for an excuse to eat french fries for dinner? Look no further. In Kenya, french fries are elevated to the status of a meal with the addition of a spicy, garlicky tomato sauce and a bright squeeze of lemon juice. Masala chips, as these dressed-up fries are known, are one of Kenyan cuisine's best-known exports and a favorite way to eat fries around the world.

Soaking the potatoes in water is critical to ensure a crisp exterior and fluffy interior. Thirty minutes is enough to do the trick, but you can soak the potatoes longer, up to several hours, by covering the bowl and storing it in the refrigerator. If you are pressed for time, try the sauce with your favorite frozen french fries.

2 large russet potatoes

3 tablespoons (42 g) ghee or (45 ml) vegetable oil

3 cloves garlic, minced

1 piece fresh ginger (1 inch/2 cm), peeled and grated (about 1 tablespoon/8 g grated)

½ yellow onion, diced

2 teaspoons kosher salt, divided

1 serrano pepper, seeded and minced

1½ teaspoons garam masala

½ teaspoon cumin

¼ teaspoon turmeric

1 tablespoon (16 g) tomato paste

2 medium tomatoes, diced

2 teaspoons vegetable oil

Juice of 1 lemon

2 tablespoons (2 g) chopped cilantro

2 tablespoons (19 g) crumbly hard cheese such as a mild feta, paneer, or queso fresco

1. Peel the potatoes and cut them into ¼-inch (5 mm) slices. Cut each slice into 4 or 5 thick fries. (Halve any especially long pieces. You're looking for fries the size of your finger.) Place the cut potatoes into a bowl of cold water and let them soak for at least 30 minutes to get rid of excess starch.
2. While the potatoes are soaking, make the masala. Heat the ghee in a large, deep skillet over medium heat. Add the garlic and ginger and cook for 1 minute, stirring. Add the onion and season with 1 teaspoon of the salt. Sauté the onion, stirring, for 5 minutes. Add the serrano pepper and spices and sauté for 3 additional minutes.
3. Add the tomato paste and diced tomatoes to the skillet and stir to combine. Sauté the tomatoes until they begin to break down and form a sauce, about 5 minutes. Remove the skillet from the heat and set aside.
4. Preheat on Air Fry at 400°F (200°C) for 3 minutes.
5. Drain the potatoes and dry them well. Toss the potatoes with the oil and remaining teaspoon of salt. Arrange the potatoes in a single layer in the air fryer basket. (Depending on the size of your machine, you may have to work in 2 batches. Do not overcrowd the basket.) Cook for 10 minutes. Open the air fryer and shake the basket to redistribute the potatoes. Cook for an additional 10 to 12 minutes until all the potatoes are browned and crisp.
6. Place the fries in the skillet with the masala sauce and add the lemon juice. Toss to coat with the sauce and cook over medium heat for a few minutes until warmed through.
7. Arrange the masala fries on a platter and garnish with chopped cilantro and crumbled cheese. Serve immediately.

Cauliflower Steaks with Tahini Sauce

SERVES 3 OR 4 ■ PREP TIME: 15 MINUTES ■ COOK TIME: 15 MINUTES

Cauliflower cut into flat "steaks" makes for a satisfying vegetarian meal any time of year. Because the core of the cauliflower holds these steaks together, you can only get two or three from each head. Save any remaining florets for another use, such as Curried Roasted Cauliflower Salad (page 58).

With the usual flour-egg-panko breading, these cruciferous steaks cook up crispy and crunchy on the outside and tender inside in only 15 minutes in the air fryer. I like to serve them with a lemony tahini sauce to give them a Middle Eastern flair, but they are pretty tasty with just a squeeze of lemon and a sprinkle of flat-leaf parsley. Sliced almonds or currants would also make a nice garnish.

Tahini Sauce

½ cup (120 g) tahini

½ cup (120 ml) freshly squeezed lemon juice

2 tablespoons (30 ml) extra-virgin olive oil

½ cup (120 ml) warm water

Cauliflower Steaks

2 heads cauliflower

1 cup (125 g) all-purpose flour

2 cups (100 g) panko breadcrumbs

2 teaspoons thyme

2 teaspoons oregano

1 teaspoon kosher salt

1 teaspoon black pepper

2 eggs beaten with 2 tablespoons (30 ml) water

Oil spray

¼ cup (15 g) chopped flat-leaf parsley

Lemon wedges, for serving

1. To make the tahini sauce, combine the tahini, lemon juice, and olive oil in a small bowl. Slowly whisk in the water until you reach the desired consistency. (You may not need the entire amount.) Set aside.
2. To make the cauliflower steaks, remove the leaves and trim the stems of the cauliflower, leaving the cores intact. Stand the cauliflower on a cutting board. Using a large knife, slice off the rounded sides of the cauliflower, leaving the middle section still attached to the core. Slice this middle section into 2 or 3 flat "steaks," depending on the size of the cauliflower, 1 to 1½ inches (2.5 to 4 cm) thick.
3. Place the flour in a shallow dish or pie plate. In a separate shallow dish, combine the panko, thyme, oregano, salt, and pepper. Dredge 2 of the cauliflower steaks first in the flour, then the egg mixture, and finally the panko mixture, coating both sides. Remove to a plate.
4. Preheat on Air Fry at 375°F (190°C) for 3 minutes.
5. Spray both sides of the cauliflower steaks with oil and place in the basket of the air fryer. Cook for 15 to 17 minutes, flipping the steaks once halfway through, until the cauliflower is fork-tender and the breading is browned and crispy. Repeat with the remaining steaks.
6. Drizzle tahini sauce over the steaks and serve with parsley and lemon wedges.

Kale and Mushroom Empanadas

MAKES 8 EMPANADAS, TO SERVE 4 ■ PREP TIME: 30 MINUTES ■ COOK TIME: 30 MINUTES

Empanadas come in many forms, both baked and fried, and can be enjoyed as an appetizer, a snack, or a meal unto themselves. This version features sautéed mushrooms and kale, so it feels both healthy and satisfying. Air-fried empanadas taste similar to baked but cook up in much less time and without having to heat up the whole house, which makes them an easy and convenient meal any time of the year.

Making empanadas from scratch is time-consuming and a true labor of love. To make these delightful turnovers more accessible for weeknight meals, I rely on frozen empanada discs, which are easy to find in grocery stores with a good selection of Latin foods.

4 tablespoons (55 g) unsalted butter, divided

1 pound (455 g) mushrooms, sliced, divided

Kosher salt

1 bunch kale, destemmed and cut into ribbons

3 cloves garlic, minced

Pinch red pepper flakes

Juice of 1 lemon

8 frozen empanada discs, thawed

Oil spray

1. Melt 2 tablespoons (28 g) of butter in a large, deep skillet over medium-high heat. When the butter is foamy, add half the mushrooms and season with salt. Cook undisturbed for 2 minutes, then stir and cook for another minute or so. Turn the heat down to medium and sauté the mushrooms, stirring occasionally, until the liquid has evaporated and the mushrooms are browned, another 5 minutes. Remove the mushrooms to a paper towel–lined plate. Add the remaining butter and repeat with the remaining mushrooms. Set the mushrooms aside.
2. Add the kale to the same skillet and sauté until it begins to wilt, 2 to 3 minutes. Add the garlic and red pepper flakes and sauté for an additional minute. Add the lemon juice and season to taste with salt. Return the mushrooms to the skillet and stir to combine. Remove from the heat and cool.
3. Remove an empanada wrapper and place it on a board. Place a heaping ¼ cup (36 g) of the mushroom-kale filling on 1 side of the empanada wrapper. Moisten the edges of the wrapper with a little water and fold the wrapper in half to form a half-moon shape. Press the dough closed around the filling and then crimp the edges of the dough with a fork to seal them shut. Place the filled empanada on a baking tray lined with parchment paper. (May be refrigerated, covered, at this point for up to several hours.)
4. Preheat on Air Fry at 375°F (190°C) for 3 minutes.
5. Spray the air fryer basket and the empanadas with oil. Working in 2 batches, place 4 empanadas in the basket of the air fryer. Cook for 8 minutes, then turn over the empanadas. Cook until the second side is firm and baked, another 5 to 7 minutes. Repeat with the second batch of empanadas. Serve immediately.

Sweet Potato and Farro Grain Bowls with Creamy Herb Dressing

SERVES 2 ■ PREP TIME: 15 MINUTES, PLUS FARRO COOK TIME ■ COOK TIME: 15 MINUTES

Grain bowls are delicious and simple all-in-one meals that allow each member of the family to customize his or her own bowl. Typically composed of a grain, such as rice, farro, or barley, and topped with vegetables, protein, and dressing, grain bowls are an easy way to create a healthy meal that feels both hearty and light.

My favorite grain bowls typically start with farro, a protein- and fiber-packed ancient grain with a delicious nutty taste and slightly chewy texture. When cooked farro is toasted in the air fryer with a spritz of oil, the grains develop a crispy crust that perfectly complements their tender, nutty interior. Top the crispy farro with air-fried vegetables and your favorite vegetable protein or a simple fried egg for a complete, one-dish meal.

Creamy Herb Dressing

½ cup (115 g) plain Greek yogurt

½ cup (8 g) fresh cilantro or (20 g) basil leaves

2 tablespoons (30 ml) extra-virgin olive oil

1 clove garlic, peeled

Juice of 1 lemon

½ teaspoon kosher salt

½ teaspoon cumin

Grain Bowls

1 cup (110 g) diced sweet potatoes

2 cups (142 g) broccoli florets

1 teaspoon kosher salt, divided

2 teaspoons olive oil, divided

2 cups (330 g) cooked and cooled pearled farro (1 cup/195 g of uncooked farro, prepared according to package directions)

½ small red onion, thinly sliced

1 small avocado, pitted and diced

Kosher salt

Freshly ground black pepper

1. To make the Creamy Herb Dressing, combine all dressing ingredients in a blender. Blend on medium speed until completely combined and smooth. If the dressing is too thick, add 1 to 2 tablespoons (15 to 30 ml) of water. (The dressing can be stored, covered, and refrigerated for up to 1 week.)
2. Combine the sweet potatoes, broccoli, and ½ teaspoon of the salt in a bowl with 1 teaspoon of the olive oil and toss to combine. Arrange the vegetables in a single layer in the air fryer basket and Air Fry at 350°F (180°C) until the potatoes are golden brown and the broccoli is tender and starting to brown on the tops, about 8 minutes. Transfer the vegetables to a platter and keep warm.
3. Drizzle the cooked farro with the remaining teaspoon of olive oil and salt and toss to combine. Cut a small piece of parchment paper to cover the bottom of the air fryer basket to prevent the farro grains from slipping through the basket holes. Add the farro to the basket and cook at 350°F (180°C) for 8 minutes, tossing gently halfway through to ensure that each grain is crisping, until the farro is crisp and golden.
4. Divide the farro between 2 bowls and top each with the sweet potatoes, broccoli, red onion, and avocado. Season with salt and pepper and drizzle with Creamy Herb Dressing. Serve warm or at room temperature.

Eggplant Parmesan

SERVES 4 ■ PREP TIME: 15 MINUTES ■ COOK TIME: 40 MINUTES

Eggplant Parmesan is typically layered and baked in a casserole, which means that the pieces of eggplant can get soggy and turn to mush. I prefer this version, where breaded eggplant cutlets are cooked in the air fryer until crispy then topped with a dollop of marinara sauce and grated cheese. The eggplant stays crisp while the sauce adds moisture and flavor and the cheese becomes gooey and melted.

Eggplant is beloved around the world for its meaty texture. This dish satisfies even the heartiest appetites while still being vegetarian.

Marinara Sauce

2 tablespoons (30 ml) extra-virgin olive oil

4 cloves garlic, minced

1 teaspoon kosher salt

½ teaspoon red pepper flakes

1 can (28 ounces/800 g) crushed tomatoes

1 teaspoon granulated sugar

Eggplant Cutlets

4 small or baby eggplants

¾ cup (94 g) all-purpose flour

2 teaspoons kosher salt

1½ teaspoons freshly ground black pepper

1 cup (50 g) panko breadcrumbs

1 cup (100 g) grated Parmesan cheese

2 eggs beaten with

2 tablespoons (30 ml) water

Oil spray

8 ounces (225 g) mozzarella cheese, grated

1. To make the marinara sauce, heat the olive oil in a medium saucepan over medium heat. Add the garlic, salt, and red pepper flakes and cook for 30 seconds to 1 minute, until the garlic is fragrant. Add the tomatoes and sugar and stir. Bring the sauce to a boil over high heat, then reduce the heat to low and simmer while you prepare the eggplant.
2. Trim the tops and bottoms off the eggplants. Cut each eggplant lengthwise into 3- or 4¼-inch (8 or 11 cm) slices. Whisk together the flour, salt, and pepper on a plate. Combine the panko and Parmesan cheese on a separate plate. Dredge 4 to 6 of the eggplant slices in the flour, tapping each one against the side of the bowl to remove any excess. Dip the slices in the egg mixture, allowing any excess to drip off. Then dredge the slices in the panko mixture. Place the breaded cutlets on a plate.
3. Spray the air fryer basket with oil. Arrange the breaded cutlets in a single layer in the basket and spray the tops with oil. Cook Air Fry at 400°F (200°C) until the top side is browned and crisp, 5 to 7 minutes. While the first batch of cutlets is cooking, bread the remaining cutlets in the same manner.
4. Flip the cutlets and spray the second side with oil. Cook until the second side is browned, another 5 to 7 minutes. Carefully top each cutlet with 1 to 2 tablespoons of marinara sauce and 1 tablespoon of grated mozzarella. Cook for an additional 2 minutes until the mozzarella is melted and browned. Remove the cutlets and cook the second batch of breaded cutlets in the same manner. Repeat with the third batch of cutlets if necessary.
5. Serve the cutlets warm with pasta and the remaining marinara sauce on the side.

Paneer Tikka

SERVES 4 ■ PREP TIME: 15 MINUTES, PLUS MARINATING TIME ■ COOK TIME: 20 MINUTES

Paneer is a firm, fresh Indian cheese that can be fried or grilled without melting or losing its shape. Like cheese curds, paneer has a bouncy texture and squeaks between your teeth. You have probably enjoyed it at Indian restaurants in dishes such as palak paneer. It is sold refrigerated, usually with the other cheeses, or sometimes frozen.

Because it holds its shape so well, paneer is a delight to cook in the air fryer with very little added fat. Here, we cube it and thread it on skewers with peppers and onions. A seasoned yogurt marinade adds flavor and gives the cooked paneer a nice char. Add some rice for a quick and easy vegetarian meal that everyone in the family will enjoy.

14 ounces (400 g) paneer

½ cup (115 g) plain yogurt

2 limes

2 cloves garlic, minced

1 tablespoon (15 ml) melted unsalted butter or vegetable oil

1 tablespoon (8 g) grated fresh ginger

1 teaspoon garam masala

1 teaspoon kosher salt

½ teaspoon cumin

¼ teaspoon turmeric

¼ teaspoon cayenne pepper

2 bell peppers, cut into 1-inch (2 cm) squares

1 red onion, cut into wedges

Oil spray

1. Cut the paneer into 1-inch (2 cm) cubes. In a large bowl, whisk together the yogurt, zest and juice from 1 of the limes, garlic, butter, ginger, and spices. Add the paneer cubes to the yogurt mixture and toss gently to coat. Allow the paneer to marinate for 30 minutes.

2. Thread the paneer cubes, bell pepper pieces, and onion wedges onto metal skewers designed for the air fryer or bamboo skewers cut to fit an air fryer. (If using bamboo skewers, soak them in water for 30 minutes prior to use.)

3. Spray the air fryer basket with oil. Working in batches, place 4 of the skewers in the basket and spray with oil. Air Fry at 375°F (190°C) for 10 minutes, turning the skewers once. Repeat with the remaining skewers. Serve the paneer tikka hot with rice and lime wedges for spritzing.

Desserts and Baked Things

I love to make desserts and sweet treats. I was a pastry chef for many years, and I tend to bake when upset; it took me almost ten years to realize my husband would deliberately annoy me so I would whip up a batch of cookies or make a triple-layer cake. I could have named a couple of these recipes specifically after a tiff or two from over the years! Air fryers are quite effective for any fried item, such as donuts or fritters, but who knew cakes and pies are exceptional in this little appliance? As with the other recipes in this book, the air fryer model will affect the recipe's time and temperature, perhaps even more for baked goods. So, tweak the recipe if the results aren't perfect, and eat the "failures" with no guilt; they, of course, don't count as calories!

Fried Sesame Bananas page 162

Southern Peach Mini Pies

MAKES 12 ■ PREP TIME: 20 MINUTES, PLUS CHILLING TIME ■ COOK TIME: 30 MINUTES

I made thousands of mini pies using every kind of fruit in my catering business years, sometimes as wedding favors. Making these golden, sweet tarts in my air fryer is quick and the pastry and filling are flawless. I am fanatical about my pie pastry being done, so I was delighted by the fully cooked bottoms and sides when I popped the pies out of the silicone cups. Try apple, berries, pear, or cherries instead of peach; just follow the recipe as written and swap in the desired fruit.

Crust

1 cup plus 2 tablespoons (140.5 g) all-purpose flour

1 tablespoon (13 g) granulated sugar

¼ teaspoon sea salt

½ cup (112 g) cold butter, cut into ½-inch (1 cm) cubes

4 tablespoons (60 ml) ice water

1 teaspoon freshly squeezed lemon juice

Filling

2 cups (240 g) chopped ripe fresh peaches

3 tablespoons (24 g) cornstarch

1 tablespoon (13 g) granulated sugar

1 teaspoon ground cinnamon

½ teaspoon ground nutmeg

1. In a food processor, pulse the flour, sugar, and salt a few times to combine. Add the butter and pulse until the mixture is a coarse meal with pea-size butter bits. Add the ice water and lemon juice and pulse until the dough starts to hold together.
2. Turn the dough out onto a sheet of plastic wrap, wrap it tightly, and shape it into a flat disk. Refrigerate for 2 hours.
3. Turn your cold dough out onto a lightly floured surface. Roll it out to a 12-inch (30 cm) round. Cut the dough into 12 3-inch (7.5 cm) circles; you might have to roll the dough out again to do so.
4. Press the dough into small silicone muffin cups, so the edges drape over the sides a little.
5. In a medium bowl, toss the peaches, cornstarch, sugar, cinnamon, and nutmeg until well combined.
6. Spoon the peaches into the pastry cups, filling them about three-quarters full, and fold the edges of the dough over so the fruit is partially covered.
7. Preheat on Air Fry at 350°F (180°C) for 3 minutes.
8. Place 6 mini pies in the air fryer basket and cook 15 minutes until the crust is golden and the filling is bubbly. Repeat with the remaining pies.
9. Cool the pies for 15 to 20 minutes, then pop them out of the silicone cups and serve.

Making Dough Without a Food Processor

Combine the flour, sugar, and salt in a large bowl and rub in the cold butter with your fingertips until the mixture resembles coarse crumbs. Add the lemon juice and then the ice water, tossing until the dough just sticks together when pressed. Wrap the dough in plastic wrap, shape into a disk, and refrigerate for 2 hours.

Koeksisters

SERVES 4 ■ PREP TIME: 15 MINUTES, PLUS RISING TIME ■ COOK TIME: 20 MINUTES

I am named after my Dutch mother's Great-Oma, Stephanie, a woman raised in South Africa who married a sea captain from the Netherlands. This recipe came from her, and I tweaked it for my air fryer and simplified the method. Traditional koeksisters, from the Dutch *koek* (cake) and *sissen* (sizzle), are braided, and my version is made into easy dough balls. They taste the same without the fuss, and the air fryer preparation eliminates all the hot oil and mess. I like to serve these on weekend mornings with a cup of rich coffee or cocoa.

½ cup (100 g) plus 2 tablespoons (26 g) granulated sugar, divided

½ teaspoon ground cinnamon

Pinch ground nutmeg

1½ tablespoons (25 ml) warm water

1 teaspoon active dry yeast

2 tablespoons melted butter

2 tablespoons (30 ml) warm milk

1 teaspoon vanilla extract

¼ teaspoon sea salt

2 large egg yolks

1¼ cup (156 g) all-purpose flour, plus extra for dusting

Avocado oil, for brushing

1. In a small bowl, stir together ½ cup (100 g) sugar, cinnamon, and nutmeg. Set aside.
2. In a large bowl, sprinkle the yeast over the water and let stand for 10 minutes.
3. Mix together the melted butter, milk, 2 tablespoons (26 g) sugar, vanilla, and salt in a small bowl until blended and set aside.
4. Stir the yolks into the yeast mixture and then beat the flour in with electric hand beaters until well mixed.
5. Add the milk mixture and beat by hand until the dough comes together.
6. Cover the bowl with a clean cloth and set aside in a warm place until the dough doubles in size, about 1 hour.
7. Punch the dough down and turn it out onto a lightly floured work surface. Cut the dough into 24 equal pieces, roll them into balls, and roll the balls in the cinnamon sugar. Set them aside to rise for 10 minutes.
8. Preheat on Air Fry at 360°F (185°C) for 3 minutes.
9. Lightly grease the air fry basket with the and place 12 dough balls in the basket. Lightly oil the dough and cook for 10 minutes until golden and puffed. Repeat with the remaining dough.

Using Yeast

Using yeast is not as intimidating as it might seem, and after you master this ingredient, you will have bowls of dough rising all over the place. You might be wondering what "foamy" means: after sitting, or activating, in warm water for 10 minutes or so, active yeast will be bubbly and creamy looking. If your yeast doesn't foam up, it is dead, and you should discard it.

Chocolate Chili Cake

SERVES 4 TO 6 ■ PREP TIME: 15 MINUTES ■ COOK TIME: 20 MINUTES

Chocolate and chili are complementary flavors popular in many treats and desserts, such as these lovely little cakes. The rich chocolate flavor is deepened by the slow-building heat, just enough to perk up your taste buds without overpowering the remaining ingredients. For the best results, stir the dry ingredients thoroughly to distribute the chili powder evenly, or else you could get hot spots in the finished cake. Serve with a scoop of cooling vanilla ice cream or dollop of fluffy whipped cream.

Butter, for greasing

½ cup (63 g) all-purpose flour, plus more for dusting

½ cup (115 g) brown sugar

¼ cup (50 g) granulated sugar

⅓ cup (29 g) cocoa powder

¾ teaspoon baking powder

½ teaspoon baking soda

¼ teaspoon chili powder

¼ teaspoon sea salt

¾ cup (175 ml) buttermilk

¼ cup (60 ml) hot brewed coffee

¼ cup (60 ml) canola oil

1 large egg

1 teaspoon vanilla extract

Confectioner's sugar, for dusting

1. Lightly butter and flour a 7-inch (18 cm) round (3-inch/7.5 cm deep) baking pan.
2. Stir together the flour, brown sugar, granulated sugar, cocoa powder, baking powder, baking soda, chili powder, and salt in a large bowl.
3. In a medium bowl, whisk together the buttermilk, coffee, oil, egg, and vanilla.
4. Add the wet ingredients to the dry ingredients and mix until the batter is smooth. Pour the batter into the prepared pan and cover tightly with foil. Poke about 10 holes in the foil all over to vent the moisture when it cooks.
5. Preheat on Air Fry at 350°F (180°C) for 3 minutes.
6. Cook the cake for 30 minutes, uncover it, reduce the heat to 315°F (160°C), and cook for 5 to 10 minutes or until a knife inserted in the center comes out clean.
7. Cool the cake for 10 minutes in the pan and then turn it out onto a wire rack.
8. Dust with confectioners' sugar and serve warm.

Pecan Baklava

SERVES 6 ■ PREP TIME: 20 MINUTES ■ COOK TIME: 25 MINUTES

I encountered baklava late in life, in my thirties, when I had to throw together four hundred portions for a wedding at our event center. I was blown away by the undeniable decadence of layers of butter, pastry, nuts, and overflowing honey syrup. I thought it would be sickeningly sweet but by some culinary magic, the squares were rich, crunchy, buttery, and just sweet enough. My air fryer does not produce hundreds of portions but is perfectly sized to put out the right amount for an intimate dinner party or to share with my husband on our back deck.

2¼ cups (248 g) finely chopped pecans

½ teaspoon ground cinnamon

20 sheets phyllo pastry

½ cup (112 g) unsalted butter, melted

½ cup (120 ml) water

½ cup (100 g) granulated sugar

⅓ cup (115 g) honey

1 tablespoon (14 g) butter, plus extra for greasing

⅛ teaspoon ground cloves

1. Lightly grease a 7-inch (18 cm) round cake dish with butter.
2. Toss together the pecans and cinnamon in a small bowl and set aside.
3. Lay the phyllo in a stack and cut to fit the baking pan.
4. In the baking pan, layer 5 phyllo sheets, brushing each with melted butter. Spread ¾ cup (83 g) of the nut mixture on the phyllo. Continue layering phyllo, melted butter, and nuts until you use up the last 5 sheets. Refrigerate the dish for 10 minutes and then use a sharp knife to cut the layers into squares or diamond shapes.
5. Preheat on Air Fry at 360°F (185°C) for 3 minutes.
6. Cook the baklava for 25 minutes until golden brown and crispy.
7. While the baklava is baking, stir together the water, sugar, honey, butter, and cloves in a medium saucepan over medium-high heat. Bring to a boil, then reduce the heat to low and simmer 5 to 7 minutes to dissolve the sugar. Set aside.
8. Remove the baklava from the oven and pour the syrup over it evenly. Let the baklava cool completely and serve.

Fried Sesame Bananas

SERVES 4 ■ PREP TIME: 15 MINUTES ■ COOK TIME: 30 MINUTES

These are not quite fritters, more like bananas wrapped in crunchy sesame honey cookies. The sweetness of the banana is balanced by the nutty, toasty flavor of the seeds. Air frying these exotic nuggets creates a lovely breading and pleasing soft texture in the fruit. It is best to wait before eating them because the sweet banana filling can be scalding!

½ cup (80 g) rice flour

½ cup (72 g) sesame seeds

1 tablespoon (7 g) confectioner's sugar

Pinch sea salt

1 large egg

2 tablespoons (30 ml) water

3 bananas, cut into 1-inch (2 cm) slices

Oil spray

Honey, for serving

1. In a medium bowl, stir together the flour, sesame seeds, confectioner's sugar, and salt.
2. In a small bowl, stir together the egg and water until well blended.
3. Dredge the banana chunks in the sesame mixture, then the egg, and then the sesame mixture again, using your fingers to press the breading onto the fruit. Place the breaded chunks on a plate until all the banana is coated.
4. Preheat on Air Fry at 370°F (190°C) for 3 minutes.
5. Working in batches, place the banana chunks in a single layer in the air fryer basket and spray each piece with oil or melted butter.
6. Cook for 8 to 10 minutes, turning halfway through, until golden brown. Repeat with the remaining banana.
7. Let stand for at least 10 minutes and serve drizzled generously with honey.

Mandazi with Chocolate Dipping Sauce

SERVES 4 ■ PREP TIME: 20 MINUTES ■ COOK TIME: 30 MINUTES

Mandazi is fried bread, similar to donuts, but lightly flavored with citrusy cardamom and not quite as sweet. This version uses coconut milk for added richness and omits the yeast for a quicker result. If you want a savory version to serve with curry or a spicy tagine, reduce the sugar by two tablespoons and use the chocolate sauce for another lovely dessert.

Chocolate Dipping Sauce

½ cup (88 g) dark chocolate (70 percent) chips

¼ cup (60 ml) heavy cream

1 tablespoon (15 ml) whole milk

2 teaspoons unsalted butter

½ teaspoon vanilla extract

¼ teaspoon espresso powder

Mandazi

1½ (188 g) cups all-purpose flour, plus extra for dusting

3 tablespoons (39 g) granulated sugar

1 teaspoon baking powder

¾ teaspoon ground cardamom

¼ teaspoon sea salt

¾ cup (175 ml) canned coconut milk

1 large egg, beaten

Avocado oil, for brushing

1. Place the chocolate chips in a medium bowl and set aside.
2. In a small saucepan, heat the cream and milk over medium heat until just simmering, about 4 minutes. Pour the hot cream mixture over the chocolate and let stand for 5 minutes. Stir until the chocolate is melted and the mixture is very smooth.
3. Stir in the butter, vanilla, and espresso powder until very well blended.
4. Pour into a serving dish and set aside until the mandazi are cooked.
5. In a large bowl, mix together the flour, sugar, baking powder, cardamom, and salt until well blended. Make a well in the center and add the coconut milk and egg. Stir until the dough just comes together.
6. Dust a clean work surface with flour, turn out the dough, and knead until it comes together and is smooth. Divide the dough into 2 equal pieces. Roll each piece into a circle about ¼-inch (5 mm) thick. Cut the circles into 8 equal triangles each.
7. Preheat on Air Fry at 350°F (180°C) for 3 minutes.
8. Cover half the triangles with a clean cloth and arrange the other 8 in the air fryer basket. Brush with oil and cook for 10 minutes until golden brown and puffy. Turn halfway through the cooking time and brush the other side with oil. Remove the mandazi to a plate and repeat with the remaining dough.
9. Serve warm with the dipping sauce.

Piña Colada Bread Pudding

SERVES 4 ■ PREP TIME: 15 MINUTES, PLUS SOAKING TIME ■ COOK TIME: 20 MINUTES

Bread pudding was one of the most requested desserts at the restaurants I worked in, any flavor or ingredients. This was very convenient because we had heaps of bread ends and pieces left over from cutting bread for baskets on the table. The base recipe is just bread, sugar, eggs, and milk—in this case, coconut milk. The added pineapple and juice, shredded coconut, and rum extract create a tropical taste sensation similar to the popular drink. You can use a half-ounce of rum instead of the extract if you are not a teetotaler.

Coconut oil, for greasing

¾ cup (175 ml) canned coconut milk

3 large eggs

4 tablespoons (52 g) granulated sugar

½ teaspoon vanilla extract

½ teaspoon rum extract

3 cups (200 g) French bread, cut into ¾-inch (2 cm) cubes

¾ cup (120 g) diced canned pineapple

½ cup (40 g) shredded coconut

1. Lightly grease a 7-inch (18 cm) round (3-inch/7.5 cm deep) baking pan with coconut oil.
2. In a large bowl, whisk together the coconut milk, eggs, sugar, vanilla, and rum extract.
3. Add the bread, pineapple, and coconut to the baking pan and pour the coconut milk mixture over, stirring to coat. Set the pan aside at room temperature for 30 minutes to soak.
4. Preheat the air fryer on Roast at 350°F (180°C) for 3 minutes.
5. Cook the bread pudding for 20 minutes until golden brown and set.
6. Cool the pudding for 10 minutes and serve.

You can also create these in mini loaf pans; two fit perfectly in the basket of even a small air fryer. The timing is the same, but the presentation is more polished, which might be the best choice for company or a romantic evening.

Key Lime Cake

SERVES 4 ■ PREP TIME: 15 MINUTES ■ COOK TIME: 35 MINUTES

Citrus desserts are at the top of the list of popular flavors worldwide because the tart-sweet combination wakes up the taste buds. This pudding uses both juice and zest of limes to double up on the intense flavor; the zest's essential oils are particularly strong, so don't scrimp on that ingredient. If you cannot find key limes—a smaller, more intense fruit— regular Persian limes work just fine. This pudding can also be made in small ramekins instead of the larger pan; just reduce the cooking time to 15 minutes.

½ cup (112 g) butter, plus extra for greasing

½ cup (100 g) granulated sugar

2 large eggs

¼ cup (60 ml) buttermilk

Juice and zest of 1 lime

1 cup (125 g) all-purpose flour, plus extra for dusting

1½ teaspoons baking powder

¼ teaspoon sea salt

Confectioners' sugar, for dusting

1. Lightly grease a 6-inch (15 cm) round baking dish with butter and dust it lightly with flour. Set aside.
2. In a large bowl, beat together the butter and sugar until fluffy. Add the eggs, buttermilk, lime juice, and lime zest and beat until well combined.
3. In a small bowl, stir together the flour, baking powder, and salt until blended.
4. Add the dry ingredients to the wet and beat until combined.
5. Transfer the batter to the baking dish and smooth the top.
6. Preheat on Air Fry at 320°F (170°C) for 3 minutes.
7. Cook for 30 to 35 minutes, or until a knife inserted into the center comes out clean.
8. Cool in the pan for 10 minutes and then pop the cake out to cool completely on a wire rack. Dust with confectioners' sugar and serve.

Rhubarb Crumble

SERVES 4 ■ PREP TIME: 15 MINUTES ■ COOK TIME: 35 MINUTES

Crumble, cobbler, brown Betty, crisp, or grunt are all different variations of the same dessert theme—cooked fruit base and a crumb topping. This version uses oats, butter, and flour to create a cookie-like covering that balances the tart stewed rhubarb perfectly. Rhubarb is a vegetable treated like fruit in most recipes, cooked with sugar to mellow out its intense tartness. This ingredient is in season in the late spring and summer and can be found in most stores looking like stalks of reddish-green celery. If you pick it from your garden or buy it at a market with the leaves attached, cut them off and discard them, because the leaves can be toxic.

¾ pound (340 g) rhubarb, cut into ½-inch (1 cm) pieces

Juice of ½ orange

⅓ cup (67 g) granulated sugar

½ cup (63 g) all-purpose flour, divided

⅓ cup (52 g) rolled oats

¼ cup (60 g) brown sugar

¼ teaspoon ground cinnamon

⅓ cup (75 g) butter, at room temperature, plus extra for greasing

1. Lightly grease a 7-inch (18 cm) round baking pan with butter.
2. Place the rhubarb, orange juice, sugar, and 2 tablespoons (16 g) flour in a medium bowl and toss to combine. Transfer the mixture to the baking pan and cover it tightly with aluminum foil.
3. Air Fry at 350°F (180°C) for 15 minutes, stirring once, until the fruit is tender and the juices release. Uncover the pan and cook 10 minutes longer. The fruit should be very soft.
4. While the fruit is cooking, in a medium bowl, stir together the remaining flour, oats, brown sugar, and cinnamon until combined. Add the butter and stir until the mixture resembles coarse crumbs.
5. Top the cooked fruit with the crumble and cook until golden, about 10 minutes. Serve warm.

Mango Turon

SERVES 4 ■ PREP TIME: 20 MINUTES ■ COOK TIME: 20 MINUTES

This is essentially a mango-filled spring roll: tart, sweet, and flavored with a hint of lovely cinnamon. When I first made this dessert, I was not impressed by its appearance, and I didn't wait long enough before eating one, so hot, soft mango burned my mouth. For some reason, I could not stop eating them once I started. Was it the crisp, air-fried wrapper, the rich mango, the interesting contrast of textures, or the warm spice? I don't know, but my husband and I ate them all, even though I was just testing the recipe. It is a delicious mystery.

½ cup (100 g) granulated sugar

½ teaspoon ground cinnamon

2 large mangos, cut into 2x1-inch (5x2 cm) pieces

12 spring roll wrappers

Water, for brushing

Oil spray

1. Place the sugar and cinnamon on a plate and stir to combine.
2. Roll the mango in the sugar until coated. Place a mango piece diagonally in the middle of a spring roll wrapper and fold one corner up over the fruit. Fold the sides over the mango and brush the last corner with water. Roll the mango to form a sealed packet. Repeat with the remaining mango and wrappers and spray them all lightly with oil.
3. Preheat on Air Fry at 390°F (200°C) for 3 minutes.
4. Place 6 turon in the air fryer basket and cook until browned and crispy, about 10 minutes, turning halfway through. Repeat with the remaining turon.
5. Let stand for 15 minutes and serve warm.

Thyme Focaccia Bread

SERVES 4 ■ PREP TIME: 15 MINUTES, PLUS RISING TIME ■ COOK TIME: 12 MINUTES

Focaccia is sometimes described as pizza dough without any toppings, which is true in essence but misses all the wonderful differences. Focaccia is pillowy, aerated with holes through the dough, crispy, and pitted on the top to hold olive oil, garlic, herbs, and other additions. It might look like naked pizza dough, but it is anything but just-baked bread. This is a simple base recipe topped with fragrant thyme, but you can experiment with other ingredients to create the ideal combination for you.

½ cup (120 ml) lukewarm water

5 tablespoons (75 ml) olive oil, divided, plus extra for greasing

½ teaspoon granulated sugar

¼ teaspoon sea salt

1¼ cups (172 g) white bread flour

1¼ teaspoons instant dry yeast or bread machine yeast

½ tablespoon chopped fresh thyme, divided

1. Place the water, ¼ cup (60 ml) oil, sugar, and salt in the bucket of a bread machine and stir to combine. Add the flour and the yeast. Program the machine for Dough and press Start.
2. When the cycle is complete, punch the dough down and divide it into two pieces. Lightly oil a 7-inch (18 cm) round baking pan and press one of the dough pieces into the pan. Lightly brush the dough with oil and sprinkle with half the thyme. Use your fingertips to make indents all over the dough and set aside for 20 minutes to rise.
3. Set the other piece aside, covered, until you are ready to use it.
4. Preheat on Air Fry at 360°F (185°C) for 3 minutes.
5. Cook until lightly browned, about 12 minutes. Repeat with the remaining dough after punching it down again.

No Bread Machine? No Problem.

If making the dough without a bread machine, place the water and sugar in a large bowl and sprinkle the yeast over the top. Let stand for 10 minutes until foamy. Add the flour, oil, and salt and stir until a thick, shaggy dough forms. Turn the dough out onto a floured surface and knead until smooth, about 5 to 7 minutes. Add more flour if the dough is sticky. Grease a large bowl, gather the dough into a ball, and place it in the bowl. Cover and let rise in a warm place until doubled, about 1 hour. Then follow the recipe from step 2.

Butternut Squash Pecan Scones

SERVES 6 ■ PREP TIME: 15 MINUTES ■ COOK TIME: 12 MINUTES

Scones are often associated with British high tea: a pale triangle that sticks to the roof of your mouth and needs to be moistened with clotted cream or flavored with jam. I have certainly experienced that scone, but this golden, spice-infused, cakey version is miles away in texture and taste. This baked beauty is autumn on a plate with bright, sweet squash, warm spices, and crunchy nuts. The triangle shape is ideal for the air fryer basket, and the even heat produces a gorgeous crust and color. If you are looking for a dessert scone, beat together half a cup (60 g) of confectioners' sugar, a quarter cup (80 g) of maple syrup, and a tablespoon (15 ml) of heavy cream to form a luscious glaze to drizzle over the finished, cooled scones.

½ cup (112 g) mashed cooked butternut squash

1 large egg

2 tablespoons (30 ml) heavy cream

1½ cups (188 g) all-purpose flour, plus extra for dusting

¼ cup (60 g) brown sugar

¼ teaspoon ground cinnamon

¼ teaspoon ground nutmeg

Pinch ground cloves

¼ cup (55 g) cold butter, cut into ½-inch (1 cm) cubes

¼ cup (28 g) chopped pecans

1. In a medium bowl, stir together the squash, egg, and cream until smooth.
2. In a medium bowl, combine the flour, sugar, cinnamon, nutmeg, and cloves until well blended. Add the butter and use your fingertips to rub it into the flour until it resembles coarse crumbs. Add the squash mixture and pecans and mix until just combined.
3. Turn the dough out onto a lightly floured surface and knead a few times until the dough holds together. Press it into a 7-inch (18 cm) round about ¾-inch (2 cm) thick and cut the dough into 6 equal triangles.
4. Preheat the air fryer on Roast at 340°F (175°C) for 3 minutes.
5. Place the scones in the air fryer basket and cook for 12 minutes until golden brown.
6. Cool for 10 minutes and serve.

Carrot Cake Apricot Cookies

MAKES 8 COOKIES ■ PREP TIME: 12 MINUTES ■ COOK TIME: 16 MINUTES

Who knew you could experience your favorite carrot cake flavors in a neat little cookie package? These air-fried cookies taste like they belong in an ingredient-stained notebook from someone's Nana's kitchen, old-fashioned, moist, and not overly sweet. The trick is very finely shredded carrot, so use the small hole side of a box grater for the right texture. But the secret ingredient here is chopped apricots that provide the alluring hint of tartness and chewiness. Don't be surprised if people cannot guess what that special something is in these golden treats.

Cream Cheese Glaze

1 ounce (28 g) cream cheese, at room temperature

¾ cup (90 g) confectioners' sugar

1 tablespoon (15 ml) milk

½ teaspoon vanilla extract

Carrot Cake Apricot Cookies

½ cup (63 g) all-purpose flour

¼ cup (50 g) granulated sugar

½ teaspoon baking powder

¼ teaspoon ground cinnamon

¼ teaspoon ground nutmeg

¼ teaspoon ground ginger

Pinch allspice

Pinch sea salt

1 large egg

3 tablespoons (45 ml) canola oil

1 teaspoon vanilla extract

1 small carrot, finely shredded

¼ cup (32 g) chopped dried apricot

1. In a small bowl, stir together the cream cheese, sugar, milk, and vanilla until very smooth. Set aside.
2. In a medium bowl, stir together the flour, sugar, baking powder, cinnamon, nutmeg, ginger, allspice, and salt until well blended.
3. Make a well and add the egg, oil, and vanilla. Stir to combine, then add the carrot and apricot, stirring until well mixed.
4. Preheat the air fryer on Roast at 340°F (175° C) for 3 minutes.
5. Line a 7-inch (18 cm) round baking sheet with parchment and scoop 4 cookies in 2-tablespoon measures of batter onto the sheet. Cook for 7 to 8 minutes until lightly browned and firm. Remove to a cutting board to cool and repeat with the remaining batter.
6. When the cookies are cool, drizzle them with the glaze and serve.

Maple Cornbread

MAKES 4 MINI LOAVES ■ PREP TIME: 15 MINUTES ■ COOK TIME: 20 MINUTES

Cornbread is a staple in many areas in the world in some variation, but this recipe takes its inspiration from the United States, the northern regions specifically. The difference between this cornbread and the Southern version is in the cornmeal and sweetness. Yellow cornmeal, fewer eggs, and maple syrup instead of granulated sugar create a crumbly, less dense, and less sweet bread, perfect for sandwiches or as a filling snack. You can add chopped nuts, cranberries, or even bacon bits if you feel like experimenting. You can also cook this batter in small silicone cups instead of the baking pan; just reduce the cooking time by five to seven minutes.

1 cup (125 g) all-purpose flour

¾ teaspoon baking powder

¼ teaspoon baking soda

¼ teaspoon ground nutmeg

Pinch sea salt

¾ cup (105 g) fine yellow cornmeal

2 large eggs

½ cup (120 ml) whole milk

¼ cup (80 g) maple syrup

3 tablespoons (42 g) melted butter

1. In a medium bowl, stir together the flour, baking powder, baking soda, nutmeg, and salt in a medium bowl. Stir in the cornmeal.
2. Make a well in the center and add the eggs, milk, maple syrup, and butter and stir until just combined.
3. Transfer the batter to 4 mini loaf pans (3½x2¼-inch/9x6 cm).
4. Preheat the air fryer on Roast at 320°F (170° C) for 3 minutes.
5. Place 2 loaf pans in the air fryer basket and cook for 20 minutes until golden and a toothpick inserted in the center comes out clean. Repeat with the remaining 2 loaves.
6. Serve warm, slathered in butter.

Q

R

S

T

V

W

Y

Z